The Illustrated Guide To Homebrewing

BY DAVE CARPENTER

CRAFT **Beer** & **Brewing**

Edited by Jamie Bogner and Trish Faubion
Art direction and design by Jamie Bogner
Photography by Matt Graves/mgravesphoto.com

© 2016 Unfiltered Media Group, LLC

Unfiltered Media Group, LLC
214 S. College Ave., Ste. 3
Fort Collins, CO 80524
beerandbrewing.com

ISBN: 978-0-9962689-2-9 (Print); 978-0-9962689-6-7 (eBook)

Library of Congress Control Number: 2016936890

Printed in China through Asia Pacific Offset

10 9 8 7 6 5 4 3 2 1

ACKNOWLEDGMENTS

I'd like to extend a high-gravity, barrel-aged thank you to the talented people at *Craft Beer and Brewing Magazine®* and Unfiltered Media Group, LLC, who made this book possible: Jamie Bogner for reality checks, Trish Faubion for grammar and fact checks, and John Bolton for royalty checks. Thank you to photographer Matt Graves for telling me where to stand and for translating my vague descriptions into beautiful images and to Austin Grippin for Making Stuff Just Happen on very short notice.

I would also like to raise a nonic pint of homebrew to...
...Jill Redding for taking a chance on me in the very beginning.
...Morgan and Reagan, who, despite having tasted my homebrew early on, encouraged me to continue making it.
...Shannon, Chris, Gong Ke, and Debbie for their unassuming brilliance and continued inspiration.
...Kelli for coffee and ideas.

Finally, a highly hopped imperial thank you goes to my wife, Ginny, for putting up with me when the kitchen resembles a chemistry lab, for giving me the space to write, for selflessly sampling beer after beer in the name of research, and for never once complaining. I'll finish mopping the ceiling and get those bottles out of the way soon.

– Dave Carpenter, Fort Collins, Colorado

Contents

Foreword, page 9
Introduction, page 10

Foreword

Learning how to brew beer should not be hard. The process, at its most basic level, isn't particularly difficult–create a sugary liquid, boil it to kill off the bad stuff, add some hops for bitterness and preservative qualities, cool it down, then throw in some yeast to eat the sugar and produce alcohol and CO_2. But volume after volume written on the subject of brewing focuses on technical minutiae and fear-inducing warnings that are enough to scare off the average would-be brewer. This is *not* one of those books.

This book was born of the idea that brewing is easy if you focus on what matters and just don't worry about all that extra stuff that doesn't get you from point A (raw materials) to point B (finished beer in your fridge or glass). It's meant as a confidence builder and visual primer for those who learn from watching, and it's the first of its kind in the world of homebrewing–a book built not from dense text but step-by-step photos of the brewing process and clear and simple how-to text that explains what to do and why you should do it.

Throughout this book, Dave Carpenter strives to simplify and explain every step in brewing, in practical terms, with techniques he has practiced as an avid homebrewer and technical writer for many years. And to help reinforce those techniques with visual examples, we photographed an entire brew day start-to-finish. The result is a book that we hope gives you the inspiration and the motivation to brew batches of homebrewed beer with confidence.

So grab some ingredients, fire up your brew kettle, sanitize your fermentation vessel, and start brewing now with *The Illustrated Guide to Homebrewing.*

– Jamie Bogner, Editorial Director, *Craft Beer & Brewing Magazine®*

Introduction

All men, even those we call savages, have been so tormented by the passion for strong drinks that limited as their capacities were, they were yet able to manufacture them.
– Jean Anthelme Brillat-Savarin,
The Physiology of Taste, or Transcendental Gastronomy

HUMANS, IT SEEMS, POSSESS AN instinctual urge to create and consume alcohol. Be it wine, whiskey, cider, or beer, our "passion for strong drinks" has defined trade routes, built empires, fueled revolutions, and effected legislation. Homebrewing isn't just about making beer: It's about embracing your nature as a fully realized member of civilization.

To which I say, welcome home. It's nice to have you.

As a former contributing editor for *Craft Beer & Brewing Magazine®*, I was honored to share my enthusiasm for homebrewing with CB&B readers. And now it is my privilege to share it with you in *The Illustrated Guide to Homebrewing*, a modern guidebook for the aspiring homebrewer. I hope your journey is every bit as fulfilling as mine has been.

Even with the benefit of several years' homebrewing experience, I find that cracking open a bottle of beer and hearing that telltale hiss remains a magical moment. Seemingly endless chemical reactions must coordinate in just the right way for great beer to emerge from its primordial barley soup, and yet they do, every minute of every day, in breweries, pubs, kitchens, and garages all around the world.

Complex though it may seem, brewing beer is actually *dead simple*. If you can boil water, you can make beer. And not just any beer. *Great* beer.

Consider the act of boiling water itself. Whether you're a student rehydrating ramen, a home cook making soup, or a Michelin-starred chef preparing a lobster terrine, the act of boiling water remains the same. The only differences are (1) how much water you heat and (2) what you do with it when it boils. You don't need to be an award-winning chef to cook a great meal at home. You merely need to create a dish you enjoy eating.

The same is true for brewing beer. Homebrewers follow the same processes as professional brewers, just at a much smaller scale (in fact, this book is organized around these universal processes). The differences between homemade beer and commercial beer largely come down to equipment and volume. If winning international beer awards is your goal, then yes, you must invest the time, money, and effort necessary to compete. But if you simply want to enjoy, pair, and share your own home-brewed beer, then you will be pleasantly surprised at just how simple it can be. It's entirely up to you.

On that note, virtually every aspect of homebrewing can be adapted to suit your personal preferences and needs. Whether you brew during a couple of free hours on a Tuesday evening or devote most of your weekend to making beer and maintaining equipment, you can fully customize *your* homebrewing process to fit the time, money, and energy you have available. As you read *The Illustrated Guide to Homebrewing*, I hope you'll keep in mind that no matter your approach, you can create great beer that you'll be proud to share with your friends and family.

There's no shortage of good homebrewing litera-ture out there, so what makes *The Illustrated Guide to Homebrewing* different? It is—simply—the most ac-cessible introduction to homebrewing available. Three important traits set this book apart from the herd:

■ **Plain English.** I break things down using everyday language that should be as familiar to painters and poets as it is to engineers and microbiologists. You don't need a technical background to brew good beer any more than you need to be an accomplished musician to enjoy an evening of jazz. *The Illustrated Guide to Homebrewing* is designed to give you the tools you need without overwhelming you with minutiae you may not need or want.
■ **Rich photography.** *The Illustrated Guide to Home-brewing* offers a visual perspective that shows as much as it tells. It's one thing to describe how wort (unfermented beer) should appear as it rapidly cools from boiling to room temperature. It's quite another to see it in brilliant color (page 58). This book ex-plains every step with vivid illustrations and photo-graphs that show you what to expect as you brew.

■ **Limited scope.** The singular goal of *The Illustrated Guide to Homebrewing* is to guide new homebrewers along the path that leads from "I like beer" to "I enjoy brewing my own beer from scratch." Yes, we'll touch on a few auxiliary topics along the way, but our focus remains always on learning the brewing fundamentals. Every chapter is designed with that purpose in mind.

This book is organized into four parts. In Part I, you'll learn some brewing basics: the eight steps to making beer; the four key ingredients for beer; and the various pieces of equipment needed to make beer. In Part II, we cover how to brew beer, taking each of the eight steps one at a time. The focus is extract-based brewing with specialty malts to add extra character to your beer. In Part III, we introduce all-grain brewing and the additional processes that entails. And in Part IV, you'll find homebrew recipes and a glossary.

As you immerse yourself in homebrewing, you'll learn more about beer than you ever thought possible. You'll discover new styles, ingredients, and techniques that will change the way you think about every beer you drink, including commercial examples. And, perhaps most importantly, you'll gain an opportunity to create something extraordinary and personal. There's real sat-isfaction in knowing that, for a brief moment in time, you alone enjoy the privilege of a sensory experience that is completely unique and completely yours.

Finally, always remember that homebrewing is here for you. Without you, there is no homebrew, good or bad. Allow yourself to experiment and, above all, have fun and make it your own. If at any point you're *not* having fun, take a step back, enjoy a commercial beer, ask yourself what you might enjoy more, and then do that. Keep that in mind, and I promise you'll love every minute of this delicious pursuit.

Welcome to homebrewing. Welcome to civilization. Let's brew some beer.

WARING

PROFESSIONAL
EXTRA BURNER

READY   ON

Part I

Brewing Basics

Chapter 1

Grain to Glass: Eight Essential Steps to Making Great Beer

If all the ways I have been along were marked on a map and joined up with a line, it might represent a minotaur. – Pablo Picasso

THIS CHAPTER WILL HELP YOU gain a solid understanding of how beer is made from start to finish. It's a map of the territory ahead that, hopefully, resembles a straight line more than it does a mythological beast, compelling as Picasso's minotaur may be.

I'm sure you are eager to make beer, but please take your time in this chapter. The fundamentals introduced here are universal and will serve you from the very first beer you brew as a nervous novice to the very last beer you brew as a satisfied centenarian (Homebrew makes you live longer: It's a fact).

I like to break brewing down into eight essential steps. From Manhattan's smallest kitchenettes to St. Louis's largest production facilities, all brewers share a common link in these eight fundamental processes:

- **Sanitizing equipment**
- **Preparing yeast**
- **Preparing wort**
- **Boiling wort with hops**
- **Fermenting wort into beer**
- **Maturing young beer**
- **Packaging properly aged beer**
- **Serving finished beer with care and dignity**

The *details* of each step invariably differ from one brewer to the next, even among different employees of the same brewery. And each step, in turn, includes a number of important tasks. But the *goal* of every step remains the same whether you're a brand-new brewer or an experienced brewmaster.

Let me, then, introduce the eight essential steps along with the goals we aim to accomplish at each stage. Remember, these will remain constant for virtually every beer you brew.

1. SANITIZING EQUIPMENT
Goal: Destroy unwanted microorganisms that could spoil your beer.

Good sanitation is a necessary requirement of making good beer; it is insurance against the possibility that some unseen microbe takes over your beer and ruins it. Our number one job as homebrewers is to give our chosen yeast the best possible chance of making good beer.

Imagine you are a kid and that you have to go to the pediatrician. You sit down in the waiting room with your mom or dad and immediately notice an Etch A Sketch® on the coffee table. In all likelihood, it displays the work of the patient who was there immediately before you. So what's the first thing you do before you can offer up your own roughly hewn, monochromatic rendition of *Starry Night*? You shake the living hell out of it and erase all traces of what came before.

Sanitation is similar to shaking the Etch A Sketch. It creates a clean slate that's ready to receive your masterpiece. In the case of brewing, the clean slate is an environment that's mostly free of naturally occurring microorganisms. I say *mostly* because it's neither necessary nor practical to create a completely sterile environment (more about that in **Chapter 4**). Instead, good sanitation gives your deliberately chosen microbes—yeast cells—the opportunity to establish themselves before anything else can. And that means reducing populations of ambient yeasts and bacteria to acceptable levels.

Seasoned homebrewers like to stress the importance of sanitation, and I encourage you to be diligent about sanitation from day one. But I don't want you to panic about your inevitable small errors, so I'm going to tell you a secret:

When you first start out as a homebrewer, with brand-new equipment and a set of deliberate step-by-step instructions such as this book, the likelihood of contamination is rather low. It's possible, but unlikely. Contamination becomes more of a problem once you've been brewing for a while. Perhaps your equipment gets scratched. Maybe you forget to sanitize it. Or your experiments with wild yeasts and souring bacteria contaminate a piece of tubing. But with your brand-new equipment and the deliberate sanitation methods described in **Chapter 4,** you'll do just fine.

2. PREPARING YEAST

Goal: Obtain a healthy culture of yeast cells that are up to the task of fermenting your beer.

It has been said so often that it sounds trite, but it bears repeating here because it's absolutely true: *Brewers don't make beer. Brewers make wort, and yeast makes beer.* If ever the yeasts rise up and learn to make wort, humans are doomed, and we'll have to learn some new skills. Until then, our job is to make wort and then give our chosen yeast the best possible chance of turning it into good beer that we enjoy drinking.

Yeast preparation is one of the most important steps in any beer recipe, which is why I place it near the very beginning. When you first start brewing, preparing yeast is as simple as heading down to the homebrew store—or clicking a few buttons in a Web browser—and purchasing a ready-to-use package of healthy yeast cells. Many homebrewers purchase brand-new packets of yeast for each batch they brew because it's convenient and top-notch yeast health is guaranteed.

If you've ever toured a mid-sized or large brewery, though, you've no doubt seen that such facilities often have entire labs dedicated to yeast management. That's how important it is. **Chapter 5** is devoted to discussing some techniques you can use at home to emulate what the big brewers do, such as reusing yeast from one batch to the next or building up a large colony from a smaller one. But know that such complications are totally voluntary: You *always* have the option of buying one or more packages of yeast and moving on with your life.

3. PREPARING WORT

Goal: Extract fermentable sugars from grain.

Wort (rhymes with dirt) is the term for yet-to-be-fermented beer. If it were possible to squeeze sugar out of grain the way vintners press juice from wine grapes, then wort would be the resulting ambrosia that drips from the barley kernels. It takes a bit more to coax sugar from grain than it does to get juice out of grapes, but the effort is worth it.

That effort comes in the form of *mashing*, which, despite the name, involves little to no mechanical pressing whatsoever. Mashing is simply the process by which sugar is extracted from malted grain such as barley, wheat, or rye. I define malt a little more rigorously in **Chapter 2**, but for now, know that malt is raw grain that has been modified to make it more suitable for making beer (or whiskey). (Beer and whiskey both begin life by mashing malted grain. And both are destined for greatness.)

All mashing means (and seriously, this is all it means) is soaking some crushed malted grains in hot water at a specific temperature for a length of time. Sometimes you have to soak it at one temperature and then heat it to a higher temperature, but most of the time, it just means adding some hot water to crushed grain and leaving it there for an hour or so. That's it. (No, seriously, that's it. If you can make instant oatmeal, you can mash grain.)

After the mash is complete, then we can drain the

sugar-rich barley juice into another vessel, where we boil it with hops before our yeast turns it into beer. But wait! There's more.

Modern technology affords us the option of either mashing grain ourselves or taking a convenient shortcut by using malt extract, a sort of ready-made wort concentrate that you reconstitute with water. Either way, you end up with wort in the end. The only substantial difference is the path you use to get there. Most homebrewers start out using malt extract because it's ridiculously simple, saves a lot of time, and avoids some potential pitfalls of mashing. (You might hear the occasional homebrewer poo-pooing extract, alleging that if you don't mash your own grain then you're not a real brewer. Ignore such negative voices, let them simmer in their curmudgeonly ways, and keep brewing!)

Some homebrewers move to all-grain methods after a while, and some don't. Excellent beer can be made either way, and I cover both extract-based and all-grain wort preparation in **Chapter 6** and **Part III**, respectively.

I brew mostly from grain these days, but about a quarter of my beer still begins life as extract, an even greater percentage when I get really busy. I recommend that all homebrewers at least start with extract-based wort preparation. This lets you focus on making good beer without having to bother with the details of mashing, kind of like learning to drive on an automatic transmission before deciding whether a stick shift is right for you.

Regardless of the method you use, what emerges from malted barley (or wheat, or rye...) is technically called *sweet wort*, which just means that it hasn't yet been boiled with hops. I use the term *wort* generically to mean any proto-beer that our yeasty friends have not yet fermented. Whether that sugar-rich liquid happens to have been seasoned with hops yet should be clear from the context.

4. BOILING WORT WITH HOPS
Goal: Sanitize wort and introduce bitterness, flavor, and aroma from hops.

Having collected wort from conducting a mash or from dissolving some malt extract in hot water, it's time to boil the wort with hops. Boiling serves several purposes:

- It sanitizes wort.
- It extracts bitterness, flavor, aroma, and antiseptic compounds from hops.
- It concentrates wort down to the desired volume and strength.
- It slightly caramelizes and darkens wort.
- It promotes clear beer.

The boil usually lasts an hour, but it can take up to 90 minutes in some cases. Occasionally you'll hear of a 2-hour or longer boil, but those are very, very rare, especially if you use extract-based wort. We cover all of the details of boiling in **Chapter 7**.

Boiling is an effective way to destroy microbes, which is one reason why travelers and outdoorsy types are advised to adequately treat or boil all water that might host nasties. In our case, boiling removes most of the naturally occurring bacteria and wild yeasts that live all around us, including on the grain itself. Boiling is therefore the final step in the sanitation process we started in Step 1, which means *everything that touches wort after the boil needs to be properly sanitized to reduce the risk of contamination.*

But it's not just about being sanitary. Adding hops to boiling wort delivers the bitterness, flavor, and aroma that are so desirable in high-quality craft beer. The longer we boil hops, the more bitterness we get out of them, but at the expense of delicate flavor and aroma compounds. Shorter boil times preserve those desirable sensory qualities. Thus, adding the right amounts of the right kinds of hops at the right times during the boil is an important part of creating the beer we set out to make.

Fortuitously, the very hops upon which we rely for bitterness, flavor, and aroma also lend antibacterial compounds to the finished beer, helping stabilize it and improving its shelf life. In fact, the antiseptic nature of boiled hops is one reason that brewers embraced hops in the first place (more on that in the next chapter).

Boiling concentrates and darkens the wort, a phenomenon you might not notice in light styles such as Pilsner. But strong Scotch ales, for example, historically rely upon an extended boil to caramelize wort sugars and create flavors that would otherwise be difficult to achieve. The turbulent, violent nature of a good rolling boil also encourages proteins to precipitate out of solution, promoting clarity.

After we've boiled the wort for the appropriate amount of time, we rapidly cool it to the temperature at which it is to be fermented. There are several reasons for quickly cooling the wort:

- It reduces the likelihood of contamination.
- It improves flavor.
- It promotes clear beer.

You'll sometimes hear brewers talk about a *hot side* and a *cold side* to brewing. The hot side consists of all processes up to and including the boil itself, while the cold side includes everything that happens after the boil, including cooling the wort to fermentation temperature. There's no need to sanitize equipment on the hot side since boiling eliminates stray microbes, but once we enter the cold side, (I'll say it again) everything that touches the wort needs to be sanitized.

5. FERMENTING WORT INTO BEER

Goal: Convert wort sugars into carbon dioxide and alcohol.

After wort has been boiled with hops and then cooled to the proper fermentation temperature, it's time for the main event: transforming that wort into beer! But this isn't something we brewers can do. It takes yeast—and a lot of it—to perform this metabolic miracle.

When the wort is cool enough, we *pitch the yeast,* which is a fancy brewing term that means "adding yeast to wort." There's nothing ceremonious or regal about it. You literally dump a bunch of yeast into cool wort. Compared with all the cleaning and boiling and running around that happens in the run-up to pitching, the act itself is pretty anticlimactic. But *pitching* sounds more romantic and euphonious than *dumping,* so we stick with it.

Over a period of days, your army of yeast cells devours wort sugars, creating carbon dioxide and ethanol (alcohol) along the way. At the peak of fermentation, a brown foam called *Kräusen* (a German word pronounced "KROY-zen") usually develops on top of the bubbling brew, a sure sign that miracles are happening within. The airlock attached to your fermentor may or may not bubble as carbon dioxide escapes from the lively beer.

Fermentation takes anywhere from 2 days to 2 weeks, but it's up to the yeast, not us, to decide when the beer is ready. The only accurate way for us to know is by measuring the density of the in-process beer. When that density falls to the value we expect and remains stable over several consecutive measurements, then we know that fermentation is complete. We discuss fermentation in detail in **Chapter 8.**

6. MATURING YOUNG BEER

Goal: Allow the young beer time to mature and stabilize.

Most brewing literature refers to the maturation, or conditioning, phase as "secondary fermentation." I

dislike this term because it's misleading: Little to no fermentation actually takes place during the conditioning phase. Nonetheless, know that when you hear someone talk about secondary fermentation, or "racking to secondary," it means that the beer is going to spend some time taking a little nap.

This period of time is when beer ages and matures, much as chili and stew improve in the fridge for a few days after you cook them. I supposed you could also call it *ripening,* but that suggests fruit or soft cheese, and it seems a bit out of place for our beer. The maturation period is mainly a period of rest in which the beer mellows out, but it's also the time to add things such as dry hops, spices, oak, and other flavorings. We'll get to those in due time—**Chapter 9,** specifically.

Many brewers will transfer, or *rack,* their beer to another vessel for conditioning to remove it from the

7. PACKAGING AND CARBONATING PROPERLY AGED BEER

Goal: Move beer into convenient serving containers and give the beer time to develop carbonation.

Packaging is the generic term for putting your beer into something from which you'll serve it. Usually, this means bottles or kegs. The vast majority of beginning homebrewers bottle their beer, and even those of us who serve beer from kegs still bottle some of our creations to continue enjoying them for months or years to come.

Packaging is also when carbonation is introduced into the beer. In commercial settings, this often involves *forced carbonation*, in which carbon dioxide is injected at high pressure directly into the beer, not unlike home soda systems such as SodaStream®. Homebrewers who keg their beer can choose to force carbonate, but there's another time-honored method that works just as well.

Natural carbonation is the most widely used method among homebrewers, especially those who bottle. Because homebrew is unfiltered, millions of live yeast cells remain in suspension even in beer that appears crystal clear to the naked eye. When we bottle our beer, we add a small dose of sugar before securing the bottle caps. Over the span of a week or two, the live yeast cells consume that sugar and create alcohol and carbon dioxide. The actual amount of alcohol produced is small and raises the overall concentration only negligibly. But the amount of carbon dioxide is sufficient to pressurize the bottle and dissolve CO_2 throughout the beer.

More than a few breweries bottle-condition all or most of their beers, and the practice is *de rigueur* in Belgium. Some brewers claim that bottle-conditioned beer stays fresher longer and that the carbonation is smoother and more pleasant than force-carbonated beer. Others maintain that CO_2 is CO_2, regardless of how it is introduced. The only thing that ultimately matters is what you like, but as a beginning homebrewer, you'll most likely bottle-condition your beer. **Chapter 10** is all about packaging your homebrew.

large cake of yeast that will have accumulated on the bottom of the fermentation vessel. Others simply leave it alone. In either case, this period is when green beer stabilizes and yeast cells clean up after themselves. A simple pale ale may need only a few days of conditioning, while big heavy barleywines may need several months, or even a year, to fully mature.

This aging period is especially important for lager beers, which derive much of their smooth crisp character from aging for weeks or months at near-freezing temperatures. Ales don't necessarily need to be aged cold, but certain German ales such as Altbier and Kölsch do traditionally benefit from a cold maturation phase.

8. SERVING FINISHED BEER WITH CARE AND DIGNITY

Goal: Delight all five senses with a thoughtfully presented glass of beer.

The way you choose to serve your beer is every bit as important as the way you choose to brew it. Would you serve a barrel-aged barleywine in a red plastic cup for your anniversary? Would you pour a light American lager into a 6-ounce crystal snifter at the ballpark? Perhaps the answer is yes to both, and if so, great (I've enjoyed barleywine in red plastic cups around a campfire)! But do take the time to consider how you'd like your beer to be presented and make it a conscious choice, not an afterthought.

Glassware comes in all shapes and sizes, and choosing the right glass for the right beer is an art unto itself. The most important thing is to make sure that the glass is clean—I mean really clean—and the right temperature. This isn't a book about glassware, but we discuss some of the most important considerations for serving your beer in **Chapter 11.**

One thing to know about serving bottle-conditioned beer is that there is always a small amount of sediment in the bottom of the bottle. It can't hurt you, but it can affect the flavor and clarity of your beer. In most cases, you'll probably want to avoid it, but there are also times when you may want to swirl the bottle and let 'er rip. We touch on both.

LET'S BREW SOME BEER!

That's it! You should now have a good overview of what it takes to make beer from grain to glass. If it's your first time reading through this chapter, don't worry if some of it still seems fuzzy. It will become clearer as we work our way through the individual steps in **Part II.**

Chapter 2

Ingredients: The Four Pillars of Great Beer

Malt is the soul, hops the spice, yeast the spirit, and water the body of beer.
– Prof. Dr. Anton Piendl. Weihenstephan Brewing Science and
Beverage Technology Program, Technical University of Munich

THE MOST IMPORTANT PART OF making good beer is to fully clean and sanitize all of your equipment. The second most important part of making good beer is to understand, and always use, fresh high-quality ingredients. Know your raw materials, and you'll forever have the upper hand when you brew.

Beer is traditionally brewed from just four ingredients:

Malt

Hops

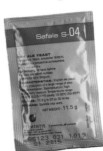

Water

Yeast

Keep in mind that these are merely the building blocks. Beer can also include spices, fruits, juices, chiles, coffee, purees, a variety of sugars, two turtle doves, and a partridge in a pear tree. In the past year, I've tried—and, for the most part, enjoyed—beers that have included basil, cucumbers, peanut butter, and even cinnamon rolls. If it's out there, there's a good chance someone has tried to ferment it (some attempts, of course, turn out better than others).

It's fun to play with exotic ingredients, but for now, let's focus on understanding the four fundamental ingredients that comprise, at least in part, every beer you're likely to ever brew.

MALT: THE SOUL OF BEER

Malt is to beer as grapes are to wine, as honey is to mead, and as apples are to cider. It supplies the sugars that yeast cells convert into alcohol and carbon dioxide. Without malt, beer as we know it would not be. It is as fundamental to ale and lager as rice and maize are to the great cuisines of Asia and Mesoamerica.

Malt is available in a dizzying number of forms, and the first time you walk into your neighborhood homebrew store, you might feel overwhelmed by the vast selection. Malts often look more or less identical and have similar sounding names, so how are you to know what's what?

As complex as malt can be, knowing how to work with it as a homebrewer really means understanding just two things:

- **Malt is always made from a *cereal grain*** (such as barley, wheat, rye, or oats) that has been *modified* to make its internal starches readily available for brewing. The degree to which a malt is modified from raw grain is called—wait for it—*modification*.
- **Malt is always kilned (heated)** to some degree. The degree of kilning may be so light as to be virtually unnoticeable or so aggressive that the kernels turn completely black. But it's always there. The degree to which malt is kilned is called *kilning* (maltsters are an imaginative lot).

That's it. Modification and kilning are the two processes that transform raw cereal grains into malt. Keep this in mind and everything else is just a matter of degree. That said, let's now take a closer look at the soul of beer.

Malt Basics

Malt is nothing more than a seed that has been tricked into thinking it is about to sprout into a new plant and then abruptly denied the opportunity to do so.

Think back to when you were in science class in grade school. Remember when you took, say, a kidney bean, placed it in a little water on the windowsill, and watched it sprout? That's really all that malt is, except you halt the process before the sprout has a chance to get too big.

Why is this important? Well, think about what a seed is. It's a small self-contained botanical package that has everything a new plant needs to kickstart its growth and develop into a seedling. Once that seedling sprouts leaves, it can make its own food using photosynthesis. Until that point, though, it needs to rely on its internal food stores.

Those internal stores are packaged as *starches*, which are very long chains of *sugars*. Chew on a cracker (which is mostly starch) for a minute or so, and once you get past the disgustingly mushy texture, you'll start to notice that it tastes sweet. That's because our saliva contains *enzymes*, which decompose starches into their constituent sugars, a process that continues when food reaches the stomach. (In fact, there's a drink indigenous to the Andes called *chicha*, which is traditionally made by chewing on maize/corn, letting the salivary enzymes do their work, and spitting the resulting mush into a pot. Get the whole village together to chew and spit for a few days, and pretty soon you have enough to ferment a beverage, which only further demonstrates the universal truth of Brillat-Savarin's assertion from the Introduction.)

Just like your saliva, kernels of barley, wheat, rye, oats, and other cereal grains also contain enzymes. And it is precisely these enzymes that allow a seed to start growing by deconstructing complex starches into simple sugars that it can use. Storing energy as starch is much more efficient and compact than storing it as sugar, so Mother Nature packs seeds full of starch as well as enzymes that the growing plant needs to convert the starch to sugar.

Yeast, the miracle fungus that makes all alcoholic beverages possible, cannot consume starch. But it has virtually no self-control when it comes to sugar. Thus, brewers exploit the natural enzymes within barley, wheat, rye, and other grains to degrade the starches in those grains into sugars that yeast cells can readily devour. For those enzymes and starches to become available, though, the seed needs to sprout, and then something has to stop it. That is where malting comes in.

A maltster first soaks raw grain in water and holds it at a specific temperature. Warm, moist conditions prompt the grain to initiate the germination process, and eventually small rootlets, called *chits*, emerge from each kernel. Simultaneously, a young shoot, called the *acrospire*, develops within the kernel itself and grows in the opposite direction of the chit. All the while, enzymes are activating and preparing to convert the seed's starches into sugars to nourish the developing plant. This process of transforming a raw seed into a starch- and enzyme-rich malt is *modification*.

Eventually the malt reaches a stage of maturity at which the enzymes are fully developed. It is at this point that the malster increases the temperature and begins *kilning* the malt. Heat stops germination in its tracks and locks the malt into a sort of state of frozen animation. Depending upon the type of malt being produced, kilning may be a quick affair that does little more than shut down germination, or it may proceed to an advanced stage that renders the malt black (and there are many intermediate stopping points as well). After the malt has been modified and kilned, it is bagged and sent off to professional brewers and homebrewers alike.

When malt reaches the brewhouse, it's ready to be used in a process called *mashing*. A mash is a thick, porridge-like mixture of crushed malt and hot water. The hot water hydrates the malt's starches and brings to life the enzymes that the maltster so carefully made available. Over a period of time, those enzymes break down the grain starches into simple sugars, which yeasts will eventually consume and create carbon dioxide (bubbles) and alcohol (booze).

Malting and mashing actually represent two steps along a single continuum, and there's no technical reason why breweries can't do both. In fact, the very largest breweries in the world actually do operate their own malting facilities to produce malts that meet the exact specifications of the brewers who will work with the malts.

But most breweries—and certainly most homebrewers—don't bother with the malting part. Instead, we purchase ready-made malt that has been produced in a malt house, or maltings, as it is sometimes called. And it is this malt that you need to decipher when designing a recipe or purchasing ingredients.

Types of Malt

Malt generally falls into two broad categories: base malt and everything else. That everything else, usually called specialty malt, is further categorized into caramel/crystal and roasted malts, so a good taxonomy for the types of malts you're likely to encounter is as follows:

Base malts, which are modified and then very lightly kilned

Caramel and crystal malts, which are modified and then moderately kilned

Roasted malts, which are modified and then heavily kilned

There are a few exceptions, of course, but this organizational scheme captures the vast majority of the malt you'll come across. In the following sections, you'll learn a little more about what each of these malt families is good for.

Base Malts

Every beer contains at least one kind of base malt. Base malt is so named because it forms the base upon which a recipe is built. Supplying the bulk of a beer's fermentable sugars, this class of malts usually represent anywhere from 75 to 100 percent of the grain that goes into a recipe.

A base malt's influence can range from style-defining to barely noticeable. A classic Bohemian Pilsner such as Pilsner Urquell (Czech Republic), for example, relies exclusively on Moravian Pilsner malt to achieve the delicate golden base upon which spicy Saaz hops are slathered. An intense barrel-aged imperial stout such as Goose Island's Bourbon County Brand Stout (Chicago, Illinois), however, includes so many specialty malts and so much barrel-aged character, that it's hard to pick out the base malt that lies beneath all that complexity.

Base malts come in all kinds of varieties, but the most important thing to know is that base malts contain enough enzymes to fully convert their own starches into sugars, and—in many cases—they have extra enzymes to convert starches in other grains as well.

Common base malts include

- **Pilsner malt,** which is sometimes called Pils malt. This is the lightest malt available. Pils malt forms the base for the vast majority of lager styles.
- **Pale malt,** which is often called, simply, "2-row." It's usually a shade darker than Pils malt, though not by much. Pale malt forms the base of the majority of ale styles.
- **Pale-ale malt,** sometimes referred to by its specific cultivar, such as Maris Otter or Golden Promise. These tend to lend a slight nuttiness or more rounded malt flavor to beer.
- **Munich malt,** which comes in varying degrees of color. These are more highly kilned than Pils and pale malts, but they still act more like base malts than caramel or crystal malts. Munich malt is traditionally found in dark German lagers such as Bock and Oktoberfest/Märzen, but it has become popular for a wide range of styles.
- **Vienna malt,** which is very similar to Munich malt. It forms the basis for traditional Vienna lager.
- **Wheat malt,** which contains no husk and is almost always used in conjunction with barley malt. German wheat beer traditionally includes more than 50 percent wheat malt, with Pils malt supplying the balance.
- **Rye malt,** which has similar properties to wheat malt and delivers a signature spiciness not unlike rye bread. Rye malt is typically used in small quantities, up to about 20 percent.

Further complicating base malts is the fact that they come from North America, Germany, the United Kingdom, Belgium, the Czech Republic, and else-

where. Each growing region contributes its own unique *terroir*, which means that Pilsner malts from Germany and the United States are likely to have a rather different taste and brewhouse performance.

Caramel and Crystal Malts

Beer brewed from just one base malt can be very good. Classics such as Pilsner Urquell (Czech Republic) and Timothy Taylor's Landlord (United Kingdom) contain nothing but Pilsner malt and Golden Promise malt, respectively. But most styles, from red ales to Doppelbocks, need additional supporting malts to add flavor, color, aroma, and body. That's where specialty malts come in. These are malts that have undergone additional processing to change their flavor and aroma.

Caramel and crystal malts usually have a glassy appearance (hence, "crystal"), and including them in a recipe lends caramelized flavors and aromas to your beer. When you sample a beer and pick up notes of toffee, caramel, raisins, or plums, there's a very good chance that you are tasting the influence of caramel malt.

Caramel and crystal malts are produced by heating hydrated, modified grain at various temperatures for various lengths of time, depending on the product being made. The simultaneous influence of moisture and heat stews the malt's starch right inside the husk, converting starch to sugar just like a little mash. The process also creates Maillard reactions, which are the same chemical phenomena that cause meat to brown when cooked in a hot skillet.

Common crystal and caramel malts include

- **Dextrin malts** such as Carapils® and Carafoam®
- **Crystal malts** numbered roughly 10–150 (the higher the number, the darker the color)
- **Caramunich malt**
- **Honey malt**
- **Melanoidin malt**
- **Special B® malt**

One confusing aspect of these kinds of malts is that every manufacturer tends to name its products using trademarks that are only slightly different from one another, often involving some riff on the word *caramel* or the prefix *cara-*. Thus, you'll find Carapils®, Carafoam®, Caramunich®, Carastan®, and so on. Fortunately, any maltster worth dealing with will also provide a numeric rating of the malt's color, which lets you roughly compare crystal and caramel malts from different manufacturers.

Special B®, for example, is an intense caramel malt from Dingemans Maltings of Belgium. It is about the same color as Extra Dark Crystal, which is produced by Simpsons Maltings in the United Kingdom. However, differences in the base malt used to produce these two products, as well as differences in malting and kilning processes, mean that substituting one for the other is very likely to yield different results in the finished beer. The beer probably won't be bad, but it won't be the same.

Roasted Malts

Roasted malts take kilning a step further. The maltster continues to kiln the malt until it starts to take on darker characteristics, not just in color, but in flavor and aroma as well. Chocolate malt, for example, has no chocolate whatsoever in it, but its taste is similar to that of dark chocolate. Black malt is even darker and is the malt equivalent of a French roast coffee: The roast dominates, leaving little of the grain's original character intact.

Examples of roasted malts include

- **Chocolate malt**
- **Black malt** (sometimes called black patent malt)
- **Various dehusked roasted malts** such as Carafa Special

Roasted barley is usually grouped in with roasted malts, but it isn't actually malted. Roasted barley is raw barley that has been roasted just like coffee. It's the signature specialty malt in dry Irish stouts such as Guinness, Murphy's, Beamish, and O'Hara's. It has the remarkable property of making a beer very dark without affecting the head at all, a visual trick that is at its finest in a freshly poured Guinness Draught from a nitrogen-powered stout faucet.

Other Malts

Naturally, there are a few kinds of malt that don't fall neatly into base, caramel/crystal, or roasted malt categories. A few that you may run across include

- **Biscuit and Victory® malts,** which are base malts that have been specially processed to deliver a toasty, biscuit-like flavor and aroma.
- **Coffee malt,** which is a roasted malt that offers up a dark color and rich flavor similar to coffee.
- **Smoked malt,** which has been exposed to wood smoke and has a pronounced campfire- or bacon-like smoke character. Peated malt is similar but has been smoked over peat instead of wood.

Maltsters develop new malts every year, so it's futile to try naming them all here. A good homebrew retailer should be able to answer any questions you have about malt.

Malt Extract

Malt extract is a convenient malt product that lets homebrewers brew beer without having to mash grain (many professional brewers admit to sneaking a bit of it in from time to time as well). Mashing is neither difficult nor complicated, but it does introduce opportunities for things to go wrong, and it takes time. A typical brew day that starts with a mash might last 5 to 7 hours, but you can easily brew beer from malt extract in just a couple of hours.

So what *is* malt extract? It's what you get when you mash a bunch of malt and then remove most of the water. Malting companies mash grain just as one would when preparing to make beer, but instead of adding hops and fermenting the resulting wort, they process the wort to remove water. The result is a concentrated wort that brewers can reconstitute at their own convenience to make beer, just as you'd add water to a can of condensed soup. Malt extract is available in two forms: liquid and dry.

Liquid malt extract (LME) is more meaningfully—but less commonly—described as malt extract syrup. It has a honey-like consistency and could easily fill in for the titular character starring opposite Steve McQueen in 1958's *The Blob*. Your local homebrew store is likely to have big plastic barrels of the stuff: All you have to do is tell them how much you need, and they'll fill a pail for you to take home and brew with. Mail-order retailers usually sell liquid extract in plastic jugs or vacuum-sealed bags.

Dry malt extract (DME), sometimes called spray malt, is made by spraying wort into a warm vacuum chamber. As each little droplet of wort flies through the chamber, the water is almost instantly sucked out of it, and the resulting pile of dry malt compounds is bagged and shipped to homebrewers worldwide.

Homebrew stores are likely to sell dry malt extract in plastic bags, usually by the pound or kilogram.

Liquid and dry malt extracts are effectively interchangeable, but because the dry product contains less moisture, you need less of it by weight than an equivalent amount of liquid extract. Dry extract has a much longer shelf life, but it comes with a slightly higher price tag. Both can make equally good beer, and the choice of one over the other is likely to come down to what your supplier carries and how you plan to use it.

Both kinds of extract are available in a wide range of styles, variously formulated for brewing different kinds of beer.

- **Pils** (or extra light) extract for light lager, Belgian golden ale, and saison
- **Pale** (or light) extract for pale ale and IPA
- **Wheat extract** for Hefeweizen, American wheat ale, saison, and more
- **Amber extract** for amber ales and lagers
- **Munich extract** for Continental-style dark lagers
- **Rye extract** for Roggenbier, rye IPA, and anything else that uses rye
- **Dark extract** for porters and stouts

A great variety of beer can be brewed by simply steeping some specialty grains in hot water for flavor and aroma and adding one of these extracts as the main source of fermentable sugars. In fact, this is the method we'll use to brew your first beer.

Adjuncts and Sugars: Not Malt, but Closely Related

Finally, let's talk just a little bit about adjuncts. In the craft-beer realm, the word *adjunct* itself is a loaded term that suggests inferiority. In truth, it's simply a catch-all for any source of fermentable sugar that doesn't happen to be malt. Most industrial-scale American breweries rely on adjuncts such as corn and rice to lighten the body and increase the alcohol content of

their products, which may be one reason that adjuncts have gotten such a bad rap.

Used in the right amounts and for the right reasons, however, adjuncts can deliver characteristics you just can't get from malt. It is worth noting that many of the world's most-sought-after commercial craft beers, including the elusive Pliny the Elder and Westvleteren XII, include adjuncts such as simple sugar.

Common adjuncts include

- **Unmalted cereal grains** such as raw barley, wheat (pictured above), rye, and oats
- **Simple sugars** such as table sugar, brown sugar, honey, and maple syrup
- **Belgian candi sugars and candi syrups**
- **Invert sugars**
- **Molasses**
- **Treacle**

There's nothing wrong with using adjuncts in your beer, as long as you enjoy drinking it!

HOPS: THE SPICE OF BEER

Malt supplies a diverse range of flavors, aromas, and color, but its number one purpose is to offer fermentable sugars. Without those sugars, there would be no beer. But hops are different. Perfectly enjoyable malt beverages can be made without them, though they're rather different from what we know today as beer. In fact, before hops became widespread, brewers in medieval Europe relied upon a mixture of herbs called *gruit* to lend bitterness and flavor to their ales, typically incorporating yarrow, mugwort, horehound, heather, and other botanicals.

Hops, however, ultimately won over brewers thanks to their intoxicating aromas and flavors and—importantly—their antiseptic properties. Today, hops are as essential to beer as malt, water, and yeast, and only a few styles continue to make use of gruit, mostly historical styles that have been resurrected as part of a broader interest in traditional styles and methods. Finnish *sahti*, for example, includes juniper berries and juniper branches in its production, but rarely does it feature hops.

Hops Basics

Hops are the cone-shaped flowers of the climbing plant *Humulus lupulus*, a member of the family Cannabaceae, which also includes species of *Cannabis*. Harvested twice a year (once in the northern hemisphere and once in the southern), hops must be dried in order to be stored and used year-round. Only so-called "wet hops" or "fresh hops" beers use hops in their unprocessed form.

We look to hops for four essential elements in our beer:

- Preservative qualities
- Bitterness
- Flavor
- Aroma

Bitterness and preservative qualities go hand in hand, for both are related to compounds called *alpha acids*. Alpha acids are found in hops resins and, when boiled in water, convert to a modified form called iso-alpha acids. Boiling, therefore, is the key to unlocking hops' ability to bitter and preserve our beer.

The act of boiling, however, also drives away volatile oils that are responsible for the unique flavors and aromas that hops have to offer. Therefore, it is common to divide hops into categories that roughly correspond to the length of time they are boiled.

- **Bittering hops** are added near the beginning of the boil, which usually lasts around 60 to 90 minutes. These hops contribute mostly bitterness to the finished beer and also help preserve it.
- **Flavor hops** are added in the final half hour or so of the boil. They still contribute some bitterness, but enough precious oils remain to lend their characteristics to the final product.
- **Aroma hops** are usually added at the very end of the boil, and in many cases, well after the boil is complete. As the name suggests, these hops deliver the beautiful aromatics that we love to sniff in, say, a freshly poured India Pale Ale (IPA).

In the past, different hops breeds were roughly categorized as bittering, flavor, or aroma hops, but the lines today are much more blurred than they once were. It is now common for a single variety of hops to be used at all points in the production of a beer.

Now let's consider a few of the forms in which you may find hops at your local homebrew store.

Fresh Cones

Fresh (or "wet") hops cones are the least processed form of *Humulus lupulus* you'll encounter. Available for a very limited time during the autumn harvest (typically late August to early October in the Northern Hemisphere, depending on climate and latitude), fresh cones are best used within 48 hours of being plucked.

The most convenient way to get your hands on fresh hops is to grow them in your own backyard: It's easier than you think (or so I am told. I hold an enviable record when it comes to successfully destroying otherwise healthy-looking plants, hops included).

If gardening isn't your thing or isn't an option, some homebrew stores now organize pre-orders and will overnight fresh hops directly to your door. But you have to be ready to use them when they arrive. Those who live near hops farms may be able to negotiate a few pounds of freshies in exchange for a day of volunteer labor (harvesting hops is hard work!).

However you acquire them, fresh cones are almost always used late in the boil to add aroma, or even after fermentation to infuse the beer with incredible fresh hops aroma. This, of course, requires a bit of timing so that the hops can go straight into the beer after harvest.

Dried Cones

Sometimes called *whole cone* or *leaf hops*, *dried cones* are fresh cones that have been dried so that they can be stored for year-round use. Properly stored, dried hops can last for several years with only minimal degradation. Some breweries pride themselves on brewing only with whole-cone hops and deploy legions of marketing professionals to make sure that consumers know it.

As a homebrewer, you'll have no trouble finding high-quality dried hops cones. Given their bulk, whole cones do present some storage challenges, though, which is why homebrewers and professionals alike overwhelmingly choose hops pellets.

Pellets

Hops pellets may not be as romantic or as nice to look at as whole cones (they resemble a peculiar cross between rabbit food and, let's say, Soylent Green?), but what they lack in aesthetic appeal, they more than make up for in convenience. Pellets are just dried cones that have been compressed and extruded through a die to create little pellets. The sticky resins within the hops are sufficient to hold the pellets together, so binding agents are neither necessary nor added.

Pellets offer several advantages over whole cones:

- Because they are compressed, pellets take up much less space than whole hops cones.
- Pellets have a lower ratio of surface area to volume than cones, which makes them less vulnerable to oxidation.
- Pellets tend to have more uniform performance characteristics than cones because the production process averages out variations in the crop.

In the end, choosing pellets or whole cones is less important than ensuring that the hops you purchase are properly stored, which means reducing exposure to oxygen and light as much as possible. Your homebrew retailer should only sell hops that are stored in the dark and that are either vacuum sealed or packaged in an inert gas such as nitrogen. Do not be afraid to ask your homebrew retailer about their hops-storage methods!

YEAST: THE SPIRIT OF BEER

The finest barley and hops in the world won't yield beer as we know it without yeast. This single-celled fungus is responsible for many of the world's greatest foodstuffs, and were all the world's yeasts to suddenly go on strike, humankind would find itself without such delicacies as

- Bread
- Kombucha
- Whiskey
- Chocolate
- Salami
- Soy sauce
- Wine
- Sake
- Mead
- Cider
- Vinegar
- Hákarl (Look it up.)
- And yes, beer

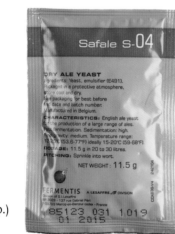

When Duke Wilhelm IV of Bavaria issued the famous *Reinheitsgebot*, or beer purity law, in 1516, the role of yeast was probably recognized, but it certainly wasn't understood. It took almost 350 years before Louis Pasteur would directly observe and describe how yeast cells anaerobically ferment sugars into ethanol and carbon dioxide.

But yeast's action is far more than mechanical conversion of this to that, and many newcomers to the world of beer are surprised to learn just how much influence yeast has upon the finished product. The signature banana and clove flavors one finds in authentic German Hefeweizen are entirely due to the yeast used. American wheat beers, though similar in other respects, have more neutral profiles because they use yeast strains that we generally describe as "cleaner," meaning fewer fermentation by-products.

Homebrewers enjoy access to an amazing array of yeast strains. The difficulty in selecting a strain today isn't finding one that's up to the task, but narrowing down the many excellent options.

Yeast Basics

Yeasts are single-celled fungi that consume sugars and create alcohol and carbon dioxide. Thousands of unique yeast species have been identified, a number that continues to grow each year. And within each species, countless individual strains have been selectively bred over decades and centuries to perform in certain ways.

The yeasts that you'll use the most as a homebrewer are of the genus *Saccharomyces*, which translates from Latin as "sugar eater." Within this genus, two species, *Saccharomyces cerevisiae* and *Saccharomyces pastorianus*, are responsible for the vast majority of ales (*S. cerevisiae*) and lagers (*S. pastorianus*) enjoyed worldwide. When you hear a brewer or a beer enthusiast talking about yeast without further clarification, in most cases he or she means *Saccharomyces*.

That said, you may have heard of—or, hopefully, enjoyed—beers that are fermented with so-called wild yeasts. Despite the evocative name, brewers commonly culture and use wild yeasts via the same high-tech methods they use for *Saccharomyces*. In brewing parlance, the term *wild* simply means that the microbes haven't been selectively pressured over the years for desirable brewhouse performance. They're less predictable—their behavior is a bit, well, wilder. Most commonly, beers are fermented using strains of *Brettanomyces*, called *Brett* for short.

Your yeast options come in one of two forms: liquid and dry.

Liquid Yeast

Liquid yeast—or, more accurately, yeast cells suspended in a liquid growth medium—is usually the least processed and most perishable yeast product available to homebrewers. Sold in plastic vials or flexible pouches, liquid yeast offers unparalleled variety and purity. Wyeast Laboratories and White Labs are the two largest suppliers of liquid strains to homebrewers, but smaller companies such as GigaYeast, East Coast Yeast, and The Yeast Bay have started making inroads in the marketplace in recent years.

Purchased fresh, most liquid yeast products supply an optimal population of yeast cells for beers of average strength (stronger beers may require using two or more packets, but we'll cover that in depth in Chapter 5). The key word here is *fresh*. Under refrigeration, you can reasonably expect liquid yeasts to remain viable for a few months, but there are many opportunities for improper handling *en route* from the yeast supplier to your kitchen. For this reason, I always keep a few packets of quality dry yeast on hand just in case my liquid culture fails to take off.

Dry Yeast

Dry yeast is similar to what you purchase in the supermarket when you want to bake bread. It comes in little sachets that typically contain about 11 grams of dry yeast. One sachet of dry yeast has more than enough cells to ferment a typical beer, and because the drying process makes yeast less sensitive to storage conditions, it's more likely to survive the journey to your house more or less intact. If you mail order your yeast, selecting dry yeast during the warm summer months isn't a bad idea.

The downside to dry yeast is that, compared to liquid products, far fewer strains are available. The drying process is expensive and time-consuming, so manufacturers only bother drying strains that are popular enough to warrant the effort. Furthermore, some yeast strains simple can't stand up to the extra bit of processing necessary to dry them. Fortunately, new dry strains are being developed all the time, and it's now possible to create American ales, English ales, Belgian ales, and German lagers using nothing but dry yeast.

WATER: THE BODY OF BEER

Good water is crucial to making good beer, so much so that entire styles have developed to take advantage of the specific water available at different brewing sites

around the world. Guinness Draught, Pilsner Urquell, and Bass Ale all owe their existence, at least in part, to the nature of the water in their cities of origin (Dublin, Ireland; Plzeň, Czech Republic; and Burton upon Trent, United Kingdom, respectively).

Water chemistry is a complex topic that warrants far more attention than I can reasonably give it in this book. We'll touch on water a little in Part III, which explains how to prepare wort using all-grain methods, but a thorough discussion is well beyond the scope of this book. Fortunately, those who brew with extracts don't need to think too much about their water. Read on to learn why.

Water Basics

Beer is mostly water, so it stands to reason that the water used to brew that beer should be of good quality. But brewers can draw an arbitrary distinction between water *quality* and water *composition*.

- **Good *quality* water** is free from contaminants and sediment, has a flavor that's pleasant enough to drink on its own, and is not heavily chlorinated. Most municipal tap water is of good quality.
- **Water *composition*,** on the other hand, refers to the relative quantities of dissolved minerals, ions, and salts. It's what we commonly think of as hard or soft water.

These terms are imprecise and, again, completely arbitrary, but they help us concentrate on what's important to the brewer. Quality is about potability and taste. Composition is about the specific makeup of the water. That brings us to a very important point:

Water *quality* is important to all brewers, but water *composition* is mostly important to those who mash grain.

Water chemistry affects all kinds of reactions in the mash, which is why entire books have been written about it. And yes, those who brew using all-grain methods do need to think about water composition to some degree. But brewers who use malt extract, especially those just getting started, need only consider water quality in most cases. Thus, brewing from extracts boils down to just two basic axioms:

- **If your tap water tastes good,** brew with it. You should have no problems brewing good beer.
- **If your tap water does not taste good** (e.g., it tastes minerally, sulfuric, metallic, or otherwise unpleasant), brew with bottled spring water—nothing terribly fancy, just basic drinking water from the local supermarket.

That's it. Nice and simple. Yes, you may want to tweak things here and there as you gain experience and discover what you like and don't like, but these simple truths will get you through the vast majority of the water situations you encounter as a beginner. In Part III, we discuss water in a little more detail for those who decide to mash their own grain.

Bottled Spring Water vs. Distilled and Reverse Osmosis Water

If you spend much time around homebrewers who've been at it a while, distilled and reverse osmosis (RO) water will almost certainly enter the conversation. You can think of these as blank canvases of more or less pure H_2O that contain very few dissolved minerals. Distilled and RO water are useful tools for brewers who want to "build their own" water from scratch, as is the case for some all-grain brewers whose municipal water supplies aren't ideal for mashing.

When brewing with malt extract, however, it's best to steer clear of distilled and reverse osmosis water because they lack the ions and minerals that help enhance flavor and mouthfeel in the finished beer. Regular spring water or drinking water contains a variety of minerals, often balanced in some way to deliver a pleasant experience for the consumer.

PUTTING IT ALL TOGETHER

Just as with cooking a meal, your beer is only as good as the ingredients you put into it. Fortunately, homebrewers enjoy access to a more diverse array of malt, hops, and yeast than ever before, and most municipal water supplies are well-suited for making good beer at home.

Every beer starts with just four basic ingredients. Use the best and freshest you can find, and you'll be well on your way to making excellent homebrew.

Chapter 3

Equipment:
La Batterie de Brasserie

A proper sauté pan, for instance, should cause serious head injury if brought down hard against someone's skull. If you have any doubts about which will dent–the victim's head or your pan–then throw that pan right in the trash.
– Anthony Bourdain, Kitchen Confidential: Adventures in the Culinary Underbelly

BREWING, LIKE COOKING, REQUIRES A certain minimum assortment of tools. And just as using a high-end sauté pan doesn't guarantee great scallops, high-end brewing equipment doesn't guarantee great beer. In the right hands, good gear can certainly turn out exquisite beer, but that doesn't necessarily mean you need the fanciest stuff out there.

Compared to other pursuits with which we entertain ourselves, homebrewing demands only modest equipment. Unlike, say, skiing, golf, classic cars, or home theaters, you can make great beer at home with only a small outlay of cash.

You may accuse me of lying if your best friend brews on a stainless steel rig with pumps, hoses, controllers, and enough power to launch half a barrel of barleywine into low earth orbit. And, indeed, there's no limit to what you *can* spend. But you don't need all that much to get started.

Any good homebrewing store should be more than eager to sell you everything you need to get you started. Most will offer a complete starter kit that includes a full range of basic necessities, usually at a favorable discount compared to purchasing it all à la carte. As always, of course, it pays to shop around.

Here are the basic items you need to get started. I describe these in greater detail as we discuss their use throughout the book.

EQUIPMENT

I consider equipment anything that has staying power, things that you buy once or very rarely. A good brew kettle, for example, might last your whole life. A plastic bottling wand, on the other hand, is likely to break at some point, or even become contaminated if it gets scratched. Thus, think of equipment as anything you purchase once with the intent of not purchasing again until the hands of circumstance make doing so a necessity.

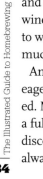

Fine mesh strainer

For removing hops after the boil.

Brew kettle

You may already have a suitable brew kettle in your kitchen pantry. All you need is a pot of 5 gallons (19 liters) or larger. In a pinch, you can even get away with one as small as 3 gallons (12 liters), but the bigger the better. Stockpots, *tamaleras* (pots for steaming tamales), and canning pots all make a good brew kettle.

Large spoon or paddle

For stirring, naturally.

Timer

If you don't already own a kitchen timer, most smartphones have a countdown timer built right in. There are also oodles of apps available that will count seconds, minutes, and hours to your heart's content.

Mesh bag

Nylon bags are reusable while muslin bags are disposable. It's worth buying a couple of mesh nylon bags up front because they have a wide range of uses and can be chucked in the washing machine and reused time and time again. Most also have drawstrings, a welcome feature that keeps floaters out of your beer.

Thermometer

You don't need a fancy thermometer to get started. An inexpensive meat thermometer is perfect because it covers the window of temperatures of interest to brewers. Avoid candy thermometers, which may sacrifice accuracy in favor of a wide temperature range.

Hydrometer (left)

A good hydrometer lets you measure fermentation progress so you know when your beer is ready or when it needs some attention. Trust me, you need one of these. You'll use it all the time.

Wine thief (right)

For pulling samples from your beer. As the name suggests, you can also use it for wine! Fermtech makes one simply called The Thief that has a unique design that lets you take hydrometer readings right in the thief itself.

Fermentation vessel with lid or stopper

Most of us start out using a food-grade plastic bucket with a lid. You can use a glass or plastic carboy, too, but you'll also need a stopper and a funnel. Regardless which you choose, make sure your fermentor has a volume of at least 6.5 gallons (25 liters). I favor the larger 8-gallon (30-liter) buckets used by home winemakers.

Airlock

This allows carbon dioxide to vent during fermentation, but prevents air from returning, which could potentially harm the beer.

Bottling bucket & wand

These are typically 6.5-gallon (25-liter) food-grade plastic buckets, just like the fermentation vessels. However, bottling buckets have a spigot near the bottom to facilitate bottling, and they rarely come with lids. The wand attaches to the spigot and features a valve that opens when pressed into the inside base of the bottle.

Bottle capper

Wing-style cappers are the most common for beginners, and they work on the vast majority of bottles you'll encounter. Bench cappers are sturdier and can cap even oddball bottles, but they are more expensive.

Auto Siphon & siphon tubing

Most of us use a gravity-fed siphon to transfer beer from point A to point B, and this handy device makes starting a siphon a breeze. The simple flexible plastic tubing lets you move wort and beer around quietly and without splashing. Make sure it's the right diameter for your auto siphon and bottling wand. If possible, try to maintain separate lengths of tubing, about 5 feet (1.5 meters) each, for siphoning and for bottling.

CONSUMABLES

Consumables are those items that you know you'll need to replace with some regularity. I like to keep a list around (I use a simple Google Doc), and every time I brew, I note how much I have left. Then I either wait or buy accordingly.

Cleaner

Avoid cleaning your brewing equipment with household detergents, which can leave a soapy film that destroys the head on your beer. Instead, turn to Powdered Brewery Wash (PBW) or good old-fashioned as-seen-on-TV OxiClean.

Sanitizer

Once you've cleaned your brewing equipment using a good cleaner, you have to sanitize it to destroy microorganisms that could potentially contaminate and spoil the beer. The two most popular sanitizers are Star San and Io-dophor, both of which require no rinsing when prepared according to the manufacturer's recommendations.

Dried malt extract (DME)

No need to run out and buy this straight away, but it's nice to keep some of this around for propagating yeast and adding additional fermentables.

Corn sugar (dextrose)

This stuff has a range of uses in the brewhouse, the most common of which is priming bottles with a small dose of sugar, which yeast eats and transforms into carbonation right in the bottle.

That's really about it. With just a few basic items, you really can make excellent beer right in your own kitchen.

And so, let's move on to Part II. In eight chapters, I discuss each of the critical steps in detail, followed by a ninth chapter devoted to putting it all together. Ready? Let's go.

The Illustrated Guide to Homebrewing

CAUTION:HOT SURF

Brewing Beer One Step at a Time

Chapter 4

Sanitation

If ignorant both of your enemy and yourself, you are certain to be in peril.
– Sun Tzu

DO YOU EAT YOGURT OR drink probiotic smoothies? If so, then you may already understand that there are good bacteria and bad bacteria. The good ones live in our intestines and help digest the food we eat. Without them, we'd be dead. Bad bacteria, on the other hand, cause strep throat, cholera, diphtheria, upper respiratory infections, food poisoning, and other grim conditions.

Similarly, when it comes to beer, there are good microorganisms and bad ones. Sanitation, the first essential step in making beer, is the process by which we destroy as many of the bad ones as we can so that the good ones, the ones we intentionally add to fresh wort, have an opportunity to establish themselves and turn that wort into delicious beer.

CLEANING VS. SANITIZING

Before we can sanitize any equipment, it first must be clean. Clean equipment is just as it sounds: It has been thoroughly washed and rinsed, and it is free of grime, caked-on gunk, dirt, fruit flies, and anything else that ought not be there. Think of it this way. If you wouldn't eat off of it, you probably shouldn't brew with it.

Cleaning needn't be a protracted chore. Just clean your brewing equipment as you would your plates, pots, pans, and other kitchenware. Try to avoid using dish soap, though, as it can leave an invisible film that may destroy the head on your beer later on. Instead, wash your equipment using an oxygen-based detergent. Powdered Brewery Wash (PBW), formulated especially for brewers, is available from virtually all homebrew retailers and is the gold standard for cleaning brewing equipment. OxiClean, another excellent choice, is widely available, highly effective, and very affordable.

In general, a good soak in PBW or OxiClean, followed by a little elbow grease, is sufficient to remove even the most stuck-on fermentation detritus. For especially stubborn grime, or when cleaning hard-to-reach surfaces such as the inside of a carboy, you may need to soak equipment overnight to sufficiently loosen the residue. Hopelessly dirty equipment may benefit from preparing the cleaning solution to a

somewhat stronger concentration than you might for normal day-to-day brewing chores. Let experience and your gut be your guides.

Glass and metal equipment can take a reasonable beating, but be especially careful with plastic equipment. Scratches can host unwelcome bacteria, so avoid using stiff brushes and scrapers on plastic pieces. Glass carboys are easiest to clean using the ubiquitous L-shaped carboy brush that comes standard with many starter equipment kits, but think twice before using such brushes on plastic carboys. At the very least, wrap the brush in a chamois cloth before going to town.

SANITATION VS. STERILIZATION

Homo sapiens is, generally speaking, a lazy species, which is why we today enjoy such modern conveniences as moving airport walkways, fast food drive-thrus, and Amazon Prime. Homebrewers are no exception, especially when it comes to the terminology we use, such as when we say *sterilization* but mean *sanitation*. The two are related but not quite the same.

Sterilization means the complete destruction of all living things. Sanitation, however, means reducing a population of living things to an acceptably small number. It's virtually impossible to sterilize your homebrewing equipment, but, thankfully, it's also unnecessary. The only time you're likely to sterilize anything is if you end up really geeking out on yeast culturing. To truly sterilize a piece of equipment usually means subjecting it to very high heat, often with superheated steam, such as in a pressure cooker or autoclave.

Fortunately, sanitation is just fine for what we need to do. Practically speaking, this means that we never completely eliminate any and all wild microbes from the equipment we use. Instead, we use proven sanitation techniques that reduce their numbers to so few that they can't gain a foothold, and the yeast we add outcompetes them for nutrients.

COMMON SANITATION METHODS

The most common way you will sanitize your brewing equipment is with **chemical sanitizers**. In the old days, homebrewers often used a dilution of plain old household bleach to sanitize equipment. In a pinch, you can still use it, although there are some very good reasons to avoid chlorine bleach unless there's no other option. Modern chemical sanitizers are typically acid-based or iodine-based, and, conveniently, require no rinsing. **Heat sanitation** is less commonly employed than chemical sanitation, but it's a good option for certain types of equipment.

Sanitizing with Chemicals

Acid-based sanitizers use a blend of food-grade acids to destroy wild bacteria and yeasts. The most popular of these is Star San, which you'll find in most homebrew stores. Properly diluted, Star San requires only a minute of contact time to effectively sanitize any surface it touches and requires no rinsing once the job is done.

Star San has a legendary tendency to foam up like laundry detergent in a decorative public fountain, and even some experienced hobbyists still get nervous at the

FIVE STA

PBW™

Not just for many household [see side]

A safe, environmentally friendly cleaner

• Removes Stubborn Stains
• Wide Temperature
• Hard Water Tole
• Easy Rinsing
• Multiple Uses

Product	Add this much sanitizer	To this much room-temperature water	Allow to soak for at least	And then
Star San	1 fl oz (30 ml)	5 gallons (19 liters)	1 minute	Don't rinse
Iodophor	1 fl oz (30 ml)	5 gallons (19 liters)	2 minutes	Don't rinse
Chlorine bleach	1 fl oz (30 ml)	1 gallon (3.8 liters)	5 minutes	Rinse *thoroughly*

sight of all those bubbles gurgling from the mouth of an open carboy as beer drains into it. But, as is commonly exclaimed, don't fear the foam! It can't hurt your beer when used at the recommended concentrations.

Another advantage of Star San is that prepared solutions can last for several weeks or months if kept away from heat and direct light. It's for this reason that many brewers like to whip up a batch of Star San in a spray bottle and spritz pieces as needed. This is especially convenient for those inevitable brief tasks that take place between brew days, when you don't have a large batch of sanitizer waiting in the wings.

Iodine-based sanitizers such as Iodophor have long been used in dairies and are just as effective as acid-based products. These also require no rinsing and are usually a little less expensive than acid-based products. Some homebrewers avoid them, though, because iodine can (and will) stain any plastic pieces it touches. I personally don't mind it: In fact, I kind of like that the inside of my fermentation bucket turns a reassuring shade of off-yellow. It makes me feel like I *really* sanitized the crap out of it. But to each his or her own.

And then there is good old household bleach. Most of us avoid this stuff because chlorine can react with some of the by-products of yeast fermentation to create a class of compounds called chlorophenols, which remind most tasters of plastic adhesive bandages. So, although bleach is an effective sanitizer, I recommend staying away from it (unless you just really enjoy the taste of Band-Aids).

If you forget to buy sanitizer and the homebrew store is closed when you're ready to brew, then by all means, whip up a batch of diluted bleach solution. But be sure to thoroughly rinse it from your brewing equipment with hot tap water to get rid of as much chlorine as you can. And never allow bleach to touch any stainless steel equipment you own: Over time, it can destroy the surface. And never, *ever* mix bleach with another cleaner such as vinegar or ammonia. The reaction releases chlorine gas, which is sufficiently toxic that it was used as a chemical weapon in World War I.

The table above indicates the proper concentrations to use for Star San, Iodophor, and household bleach, as well as how much contact time is needed and whether rinsing is required.

Sanitizing with Heat

Of course, chemicals aren't the only way to sanitize your gear. Heat does a mighty fine job as well, which is the big reason travelers are advised to boil suspect water in countries that may not enjoy all of the benefits of modern sanitation. Boiling water for just a couple of minutes kills anything that might be lurking on the surface.

You obviously don't want to boil plastic pieces such as airlocks. I mean, you *could*, but then you'd just end up with a little wad of plastic that won't get you very far on brew day. Certain glass and metal pieces of brew gear, though, can be heat treated by boiling:

- **Immersion wort chillers (right),** which are usually made from copper or stainless steel, are customarily dunked into boiling wort for 10 to 15 minutes to sanitize them. We discuss wort chillers in Chapter 7.
- **Stainless steel diffusion stones** (see Chapter 8), which some brewers use to inject oxygen into fresh wort, are effectively sanitized using a good rolling boil of tap water.
- **Borosilicate flasks** (more on those in the next chapter) can be heated right on top of a gas range with a malt extract solution as the first step in propagating yeast.

Glass bottles are probably the most amenable to heat sanitation. If you start them in a *cold* oven, turn the heat to 350°F (that's gas mark 4 in the United Kingdom, Thermostat 6 in France, Stufe 2 in Germany, and 180°C everywhere else) and leave them for an hour, you'll end up with sanitary bottles. Let them cool for half an hour or more, and then they're ready to receive your homebrewed creations.

Particularly convenient are dishwashers that feature a sanitation cycle. This is the method by which I sanitize all of my glass bottles, and I have enjoyed consistently good results. Truth be told, my dishwasher doesn't have a specific cycle marked sanitation, but it creates enough steam that I feel it's close enough. It's up to you whether that's an acceptable risk. It is for me, and I've had no issues, but your mileage may vary.

When using a dishwasher to sanitize **already clean** glass or metal gear, run it *without detergent* on the hottest cycle available, and use the hottest drying setting. Do not use the dishwasher to clean gear, only to sanitize it. Cleaning is best done by hand, as dishwasher detergent presents many of the same head-retention problems as household soap. And running your brew gear through a load with last night's caked-on lasagna is clearly a bad idea, so just stick to the sink for cleaning and let a detergent-free dishwasher handle sanitation.

MOVING ON

Maintaining good sanitation practices is the most important thing you can do to ensure reliably tasty homebrew. Take the time to adequately clean and sanitize each piece of equipment you own and don't be afraid to throw out, recycle, or repurpose pieces of gear that are well-worn and may harbor bacteria. You'll be doing yourself and your brewer's yeast a big favor.

Chapter 5

Yeast Preparation

O thou invisible spirit of wine, if thou hast no name to be known by, let us call thee devil! – Cassio, William Shakespeare's Othello

WE HUMANS HAVE ENJOYED ALCOHOLIC beverages for millennia, but our grasp of yeast's role in fermentation goes back a mere 150 years. In that century and a half, though, scientists, brewers, and bakers have made enormous strides. While our understanding of fermentation remains incomplete, we know enough to reliably and repeatedly coax favorable results from yeast (*Saccharomyces*, at least).

Yeast preparation, which you'll recall from Chapter 1 is the second essential step in making beer, is the generic term that encompasses whatever means you use to ensure that, come brew day, you have a healthy population of yeast cells that are ready to turn wort into beer. Several ways one can do this, roughly in order from easiest to hardest, include the following:

- Purchase one or more packages of liquid or dry yeast and add it to the wort.
- Purchase a package of liquid yeast, grow it into a larger culture, and add that to the wort.
- Take a portion of yeast left over from another batch of beer and add it to the wort.
- Take the dregs from the bottom of a can or bottle of unfiltered, unpasteurized beer (commercial or homebrew), grow it into a larger culture, and add that to the wort.

Yeast is the only beer ingredient that makes more of itself, and you can use this convenient fact to your advantage and reuse yeast time and time again if you want. However, until you have a few batches under your belt (and perhaps even well thereafter), I recommend taking the path of least resistance.

Purchasing fresh packets of liquid or dry yeast every time you brew guarantees that you have a healthy colony of yeast cells, which reduces the likelihood of infected beer or stalled fermentation. Most professional brewers reuse (or, in brew-speak, *re-pitch*) yeast from one batch to another, but I've spoken with many who procure fresh yeast each and every time they brew.

Check Out Receipt

NOPL at Cicero
315-699-2032
www.nopl.org

Saturday, May 20, 2023
1:08:31 PM
86747

Title: The illustrated guide to
home brewing
Material: Book
Due: 6/10/2023

Total items: 1

You just saved $24.99 by
using your library. You have
saved $24.99 this past year
and $24.99 since you began
using the library!

SUGGESTED LIQUID YEAST STRAINS FOR BEER STYLES

Beer style	Suggested Wyeast strains	Suggested White Labs strains	Other strains
English ales	1028 London Ale 1098 British Ale 1469 West Yorkshire Ale	WLP002 English Ale WLP007 English Dry WLP009 Australian Ale As the name suggests, WLP009 is well-suited to Australian sparkling ales, but it's also an excellent choice for malt-focused English styles such as ESB, brown ale, and mild ale. WLP013 London Ale	
Irish and Scottish ales	1084 Irish Ale 1728 Scottish Ale	WLP004 Irish Ale WLP023 Burton Ale	
American ales	1056 American Ale 1272 American Ale II 1450 Denny's Favorite	WLP001 California Ale WLP028 Edinburgh Scottish Ale	**East Coast Yeast** ECY10 Old Newark Ale **GigaYeast** GY054 Vermont IPA **The Yeast Bay** Vermont Ale
Belgian ales	1214 Belgian Abbey 3787 Trappist High Gravity 3944 Belgian Witbier	WLP400 Belgian Wit WLP500 Monastery Ale WLP530 Abbey Ale	
Saison	3711 French Saison	WLP566 Belgian Saison II	

I don't recommend that beginners ferment saisons with Wyeast 3724 Belgian Saison or White Labs WLP565 Belgian Saison I because these strains can be rather finicky. The indicated strains are much easier to work with and shouldn't give you any issues.

German Hefeweizen	3068 Weihenstephan Weizen 3638 Bavarian Wheat	WLP300 Hefeweizen Ale WLP351 Bavarian Weizen	
Lagers	2007 Pilsen Lager 2124 Bohemian Lager 2308 Munich Lager	WLP820 Oktoberfest/Märzen Lager WLP835 German Lager X (At press time, this excellent lager yeast was available only seasonally. It's a great strain. Let's hope it becomes a year-round offering soon!) WLP840 American Lager WLP850 Copenhagen Lager	
Kölsch and Altbier	1007 German Ale 2565 Kölsch	WLP029 German Ale/Kölsch WLP036 Düsseldorf Alt	
California common	2112 California Lager	WLP810 San Francisco Lager	

LIQUID AND DRY YEASTS

Homebrewers today have more yeast choices than ever before, and growth seems unlikely to slow down. As homebrewing's popularity increases, new yeast manufacturers are popping up here and there, and established suppliers are upping their game, expanding their offerings, and delivering more strains than you're likely to ever need.

As we discussed in Chapter 2, yeast is available to homebrewers in two forms: liquid and dry. Both are excellent, and both will make great beer if treated well and used properly. More strains are available in liquid form than in dry, but dry yeast has a longer shelf life and is easier to use for spur-of-the-moment brewing. Ultimately, the choice of one over the other depends upon your personal preferences.

Liquid Yeast

Liquid yeast products contain a liquid growth medium in which billions of yeast cells are suspended. These products are perishable and best used fresh, although making a starter (more on that soon) can boost the viability of old cultures. The two largest suppliers of liquid yeast products, White Labs and Wyeast Laboratories, collectively offer hundreds of strains of *Saccharomyces* (conventional brewer's yeast), *Brettanomyces* (wild yeast), and bacterial cultures of *Lactobacillus* and *Pediococcus* bacteria for sour ales.

Smaller suppliers such as GigaYeast, East Coast Yeast, The Yeast Bay, and Imperial Organic Yeast sell some harder-to-find products, including The Alchemist's so-called "Conan" strain and a strain said to originate from the old Ballantine brewery. You'll also find esoteric blends of bacteria and wild yeasts should your homebrewing journey take you into sour territory.

The vast array of liquid yeast strains is growing all the time, and attempting to classify them all here is pointless. However, the table on page 45 is a good starting place for brewing a variety of styles. The suggestions offered here are generally well-behaved yeasts that don't require much special treatment.

Because liquid yeast products are perishable, they must be *transported and stored under refrigeration and used as soon as possible.* If you have fresh, well-treated liquid yeast, using it couldn't be easier. You simply take it out of the refrigerator a few hours before you need it. When you're ready to pitch the yeast, you open the yeast packet and pour the contents directly into fresh wort.

SUGGESTED DRY YEAST STRAINS FOR BEER STYLES

Manufacturer	Product	Description
Fermentis	Safale US-05	American ale yeast
	Safale S-04	English ale yeast
	Safbrew WB-06	Bavarian wheat beer yeast
	Safbrew Abbaye	Belgian abbey style yeast
	Saflager W-34/70	All-purpose lager yeast
Lallemand	Danstar Belle Saison	Belgian saison yeast
	Danstar BRY-97	American ale yeast
	Danstar Nottingham	Neutral English yeast
	Danstar Windsor	Fruity English yeast
Mangrove Jack's	M27 Belgian Ale	Belgian saison yeast
	M84 Bohemian Lager	All-purpose lager yeast
	M07 British Ale	Dry English ale yeast
	M79 Burton Union	English ale yeast
	M03 Newcastle Dark Ale	Malty British ale yeast

Dry Yeast

Despite all of the wonderful and diverse liquid strains available, more often than not, I use dry yeast. There are certainly beer styles for which I prefer the liquid options that are available, but for the vast majority of English- and American-inspired ales, and even Continental lagers, dry-yeast products exist that are just as good as their liquid counterparts. Dry yeast stays viable for long periods of time, takes up very little room in the refrigerator, and can be used at the last minute.

I enjoy brewing lagers, and making a great lager means using several packets of liquid yeast or growing a large yeast population using a starter. And I do this several times a year, but it requires some planning to either buy fresh yeast or prepare a starter. However, one of the most widely used lager yeasts in the world, Weihenstephan W 34 / 70, is available as a dry product, which means I can keep a few packets in the fridge and choose to brew on a random Sunday afternoon with little to no planning. Two packets of W 34 / 70 added to 5 gallons (19 liters) of Pilsner wort are enough to get it up and running quickly and conveniently.

The quality and selection of dry yeast have dramatically improved in just the past five years, and there's every reason to believe that they will continue to do so. Some of today's most popular dry yeast products are listed in the table on page 47.

YEAST METABOLISM

You don't need a PhD in microbiology to work effectively with yeast. However, recognizing the three phases of yeast activity will help you more effectively understand what to expect from fermentation.

After you pitch, or add, yeast to fresh wort, you can expect three distinct phases:

- **Lag phase**
- **Growth phase**
- **Stationary phase**

Lag Phase

The *lag phase* is a period of what appears to the naked eye to be total inactivity; it takes place for several hours after yeast is added to fresh wort. But even though there's nothing to see, the yeast is very much active. The lag phase is similar to changing time zones or elevation: A rapid transition from one environment to another takes a bit of getting used to.

Much of a beer's character is determined during the lag phase as yeast cells absorb nutrients from the wort and prepare for growth. Most importantly, yeast needs oxygen to effectively prepare for the fermentation to come, which is why we will stress over and over the importance of introducing oxygen into wort before pitching yeast. The lag phase usually takes anywhere from 12 to 48 hours.

Growth Phase

The *growth phase* is what most of us recognize as "active fermentation." This is when yeast rapidly consumes sugar and converts it to carbon dioxide and alcohol. It's also the most visually interesting phase of the fermentation cycle. A thick, fluffy white foam (*Kräusen*) appears on top of the beer, flecked with brown bits of hops and other wort sediment.

If you ferment your beer in a transparent vessel such as a carboy, you will observe streams of carbon dioxide bubbles rising up the sides during the growth phase, and the airlock will release gas in a seemingly never-ending stream of burps. You may also notice some slight sulfur (rotten egg) aromas coming from the airlock. Some yeasts do this more than others, and it's perfectly normal.

Stationary Phase

The *stationary phase* marks the end of fermentation, when activity slows and yeast cells *flocculate*. Flocculation is the tendency for yeast cells to clump together. When the clumps reach critical mass, they drop to the bottom of the fermentor, leaving behind clear, or *bright*, beer. Some yeast strains flocculate more than others: British ale strains readily clump together (sometimes to the point of not finishing the job!), while German Hefeweizen yeast likes to remain in suspension. Flocculation is generally considered the end of fermentation, but flavors may continue to evolve for some time.

YEAST PROPAGATION

Yeast propagation is a method by which you can grow larger colonies of yeast from smaller ones. Those small colonies may be a packet of liquid yeast, the dregs at the bottom of an unfiltered commercial beer, or even a sample you receive from your local brewpub. It's generally not advisable to propagate dry yeast because dry yeast is packed with the nutrients it needs to ferment beer, and it's better to put those nutrients to work in your actual beer instead of a propagation step. Homebrewers usually call yeast propagation "making a yeast starter."

A *yeast starter* is a small volume of wort whose purpose is to give yeast cells an opportunity to reproduce. To make a starter, you prepare low-gravity wort by boiling dry malt extract (DME) with water. You then cool the wort to room temperature and pitch a packet of liquid yeast. Over the course of a couple of days, the yeast reproduces and yields a much larger population than you started with.

Full instructions on preparing a yeast starter are provided in Chapter 12 in the sidebar "How to Make a Yeast Starter," (page 84).

MOVING ON

Pitching a large population of healthy yeast cells at the right temperature can make the difference between beer that is just okay and beer that is truly remarkable. Take the time to experiment with both liquid and dry yeast strains, and don't be afraid to make substitutions if the exact strain you want is unavailable.

Homebrewing is about having fun, so choose the yeast-preparation method that is most fun for you. If you want to geek out on yeast and make a yeast starter, great! But if buying a couple of packs of fresh yeast and calling it a day is more your style, you're in good company. Increasing numbers of professional brewers do just that.

Chapter 6

Wort Preparation

*Here were also wheat, barley, and beans, and barleywine in large bowls.
Floating on the top of this drink were the barley-grains.* – Xenophon, Anabasis

WORT PREPARATION, THE THIRD ESSENTIAL step in making beer, is the central feature that distinguishes beer from other fermented beverages. To make wine, you crush grapes. To make cider, you crush apples. To make mead, you dissolve honey in water. And to make beer, you prepare wort.

Wort preparation is the process by which a brewer coaxes fermentable sugars from malted grain. In Part III, I offer an accessible introduction to what homebrewers commonly call *all-grain brewing.* Yes, technically, *all* beer is brewed from grain because, well, that's kind of the definition of beer. What *all-grain* means to homebrewers, though, is that you actually mash grain at home to get at the fermentable sugars.

In this chapter, though, we focus on brewing from malt extract with specialty grains. Why? Because it's much less time-consuming than all-grain methods. Rather than mash grain as part of your brew day, you simply dissolve malt extract, which is nothing more than wort that has been prepared from mashed grain and then concentrated down to an extract that is easy to use.

IN DEFENSE OF MALT EXTRACT–A RANT

Some things in life are virtually guaranteed. Professional athletes will always make too much money.

Flying coach will always be uncomfortable. And, at some point, if you brew from malt extract, another homebrewer will dismiss you and claim that all-grain methods are somehow superior.

Ignore him or her. Or, if you can't, then at least ask whether (s)he grows high-protein wheat, mills it into flour, prepares fresh dough, and extrudes it into fun shapes every time (s)he has a hankering for pasta. Arguing that using malt extract is in some way inferior to mashing grain is just as illogical.

Think of all of the convenience products we enjoy in our everyday lives. Do you grow your own produce? Do you make your own shampoo? Do you build your own furniture? Do you personally design and print every jigsaw puzzle you assemble?

If so, then I salute you and hope we have a chance to meet in the two or three free minutes you enjoy each month. If, however, you lead a busy life, then convenience products are probably an essential part of your existence. There's nothing inherently good or bad about all-grain methods or brewing from malt extract. They're simply different paths to the same end. What matters most is that *you* enjoy the beer you brew. Not your friends. Not your spouse. And certainly not a snotty beer judge. If you like drinking the beer you make, then you're doing it right.

Never forget that homebrewing is supposed to be *fun*. If you're not having fun, you're doing it wrong. Sometimes my idea of fun is spending most of a Saturday mashing grain, boiling wort, drinking homebrew, and being a beer geek. But it's also fun to take a walk, visit a museum, go on a date, or read a book. Malt extract frees up enough time that a busy person can both make beer *and* enjoy other aspects of a fully engaged life, including drinking said beer.

I brewed my first twenty or so batches of homebrew from malt extract and later added all-grain methods to my repertoire because I wanted to learn more about beer and get my hands dirty. That's it. But I also enjoy roasting coffee, baking sourdough bread, hacking my Android device, and dabbling in such imminently practical languages as Icelandic. I would never presume that you ought to share those same interests. (Should you desire a rich and varied social life, I would, in fact, actively discourage it.)

All of this is to say that homebrewing can expand or contract to be as casual or all-consuming as you'd like to make it. Malt extract is a handy product that makes homebrewing more approachable to a broader group of people than it would be if we all had to mash grain every time we want to make beer.

Malt extract has advantages and disadvantages just like everything else. What matters is that we acknowledge those limitations and benefits and proceed according to what matters most to us. End of rant. Let's continue.

STEEPING SPECIALTY GRAINS

As we discussed in Chapter 2, there are several types of malt, and we can generally divide them into *base malts* and *specialty malts*. While base malts supply most of a beer's fermentable sugars, specialty malts enhance color, flavor, and aroma. And even when most of a beer's fermentable sugars come from malt extract, specialty grains still offer a good deal of character.

One particularly advantageous quality of specialty grains is that they don't usually need to be mashed to access their goodness. The process of making them special does a pretty good job of converting their internal starches to water-soluble sugars, which means that most specialty grains need only be steeped in hot water to gain the color, flavor, and aroma they have to offer.

This has enormous implications for the extract brewer because specialty grains steeped in hot water will perform much the same as if they were mashed with base malt—not identically, but rather similarly. *So*, if you brew beer from extract, steeping specialty grains is an excellent way to add fresh malt character to your beer. Here's how to do it.

■ **Crush the specialty grains.** The homebrew store can do this for you, or you can crush them at home. A malt mill is ideal, but if you don't own one, a rolling pin, wine bottle, or even jumping up and

down on a grain-filled trash bag can be quite effective. All you really want to do is break up the kernels a bit. You don't need to make flour, you just need to crack open the kernels.

■ **Put the crushed grain in a mesh bag.** Muslin and nylon bags work great. You just need a mesh bag that can stand up to some heat and allow a little flow in and out. It's often convenient to tie the top of the bag into a knot to keep grain from floating away during the steep.

■ **Plop the grain-filled bag into hot water.** How hot is hot? Generally about 150–160°F (66–71°C). I usually heat my water to 160°F (71°C) and then kill the heat and drop in the grain. The temperature drops a few degrees and stabilizes, and it's perfect for this approach.

■ **Wait half an hour.** After you've added your crushed grain in a bag to the hot water, set a timer for 30 minutes and let the grain steep. Some homebrewers even add the bag of grain to the steeping water before turning on the heat and count the warm-up time toward the half hour of steeping. Either approach is effective.

■ **Pull the bag out and drain it for a bit.** Once time is up, just lift the grain bag out of the steeping water and hold it above the kettle for a bit to allow the goodness to drip into your soon-to-be wort. But

please do not squeeze the bag of grain. Squeezing has the potential to force some unwanted compounds out of the grain and into your beer. So be content to simply let the bag drip.

ADDING EXTRACT

When the steep is complete, it's time to crank up the heat to full whack and bring that barley water to a boil. Once it starts to bubble, kill the heat. It's important to add extract *off the heat*. Here's why:

■ **Liquid malt extract (LME)** is dense and will tend to sink to the bottom of the kettle. A high sugar concentration along with direct heat is a recipe for *scorching*, which does not make good beer. So kill the heat before you add your liquid malt extract.

■ **Dry malt extract (DME)** is extraordinarily hydrophilic, which means that it readily takes on water. It's so eager to do so that it forms unwieldy clumps the minute it even enters the same time zone as hot water. Take a little time to whisk it around and dissolve it somewhat before beginning the boil in earnest, lest you end up with a volcanic eruption. So kill the heat before you add your dry malt extract.

With the heat off, add your extract and stir until you have a nice, uniform liquid. This may take some time, so be patient. Once it seems pretty well mixed, congratulations, you are now the proud parent of newborn wort! Smoke a cigar, kick the heat back into high gear, and get ready for the next step: The boil!

MOVING ON

Wort preparation has the potential to be lengthy and involved or brief and simple. There's nothing inherently wrong with either approach, and I encourage you to experiment with both extract and all-grain methods. Then choose what works best for you. When you first get started, working with extract frees you to focus on the brewing process itself. You always have the option of mashing grain at a later time, if you so desire.

Or not!

Chapter 7

Boiling Wort with Hops

Double, double toil and trouble / Fire burn, and cauldron bubble.
– The Witches, William Shakespeare's Macbeth

THE BOIL, THE FOURTH ESSENTIAL step in brewing beer, is the main event on brew day. This is where newborn wort reaches its full potential and becomes fully developed yeast food. If you brew indoors on your kitchen stove, your house fills with the heady aromas of malt and hops. If you brew outdoors on a propane burner, you find yourself drawn to the brew kettle, as if it's some kind of mystical cauldron. And, in some ways, it is.

For, you see, magic happens during *the boil*. Hops yield their full complement of bitterness, flavor, and aroma. Suspended proteins that might otherwise contribute to haze clump together and drop out of solution. Heat sterilizes the wort, making it a suitable growth medium for the yeast culture to come. And volatile compounds with scary names such as dimethyl sulfide (DMS) waft away on currents of heat.

Yes, the boil is magic, indeed.

HOT BREAK AND BOILOVERS

At the end of the previous chapter, you turned the heat under your wort back on to full blast. As the wort gets hot, you'll notice a few signs that it's about to hit the boiling point.

- A thick whitish or brownish cap of foam develops on the surface of the wort.
- This cap of foam grows and rises toward the top of the kettle.
- Brown flecks appear atop the rising cap of foam.

All of these signs are your cues to keep one hand on the burner valve and the other on a spray bottle of water, set to fine mist.

The brown cap that forms on top of the rapidly warming wort is called *hot break*. It's a mishmash of proteins and sugars that has but one job: valiantly attempting to boil right the hell over the side of your boil kettle and upset your domestic partner. It is your job, as a homebrewer, to prevent it from doing so. Every one of us experiences a boilover at some point (it's kind of like death and taxes), but you have two strategies to keep that hot break contained.

First of all, you can drop the heat. The disadvantage of this approach is that you might not be able to do so quickly enough, and that's where the second part comes in: You can spray the hot break with a few fine mists of cold water. This cools down the hot break enough to make it fall back on itself.

Between lowering the flame and spritzing the wort with cold water, you should be able to manage the hot break. Eventually, it will settle down and fall back onto the boiling wort, forming a raft of foam that playfully dances on top.

Some instructions tell you to start your timer and begin adding hops as soon as the wort starts to boil. I recommend that you instead wait 5 minutes before you decree that the boil to be "officially" underway. This gives it an opportunity to stabilize and settle into its groove before you begin adding hops, which will only further infuriate it.

ADDING HOPS TO WORT

Hops do several things in beer:

- They create bitterness.
- They add flavor and aroma.
- They serve as natural antimicrobials and preservatives.
- They look pretty.

Actually, only freshly plucked green hops look pretty. The rest either resemble rabbit food or those pressed flowers you used to make during your angsty youthful phase as you attempted, unsuccessfully, to woo the object of your affections. But the first three contributions are vital, and the whole point of boiling can largely be traced to these. Generally speaking, two axioms govern hops additions.

- **The more you boil hops, the more bitterness you extract from them.**
- **The less you boil hops, the more flavor and aroma you extract from them.**

Thus, in a typical 1-hour boil, hops that are added 30 to 60 minutes before the end of the boil mainly contribute bitterness. Hops added 15 to 30 minutes before

you kill the heat tend to add flavor. And those added in the final 15 minutes offer mostly aroma.

These aren't discrete windows, and in reality, every hops addition adds some bitterness, some flavor, and some aroma. Brewers manipulate the relative contributions of these qualities by adjusting the timing of the hops additions.

Hops additions are *always* specified in terms of the amount of time before the end of the boil. Thus, all additions can be viewed as a sort of NASA-style countdown.

- A 60-minute addition is added at T-minus 60 minutes.
- A 15-minute addition is added at T-minus 15 minutes.
- A 0-minute addition is added at liftoff, or, as brewers call it, *flameout* or *knockout*.

There are also some hops additions that are added well into the mission, usually at about T-plus 14 days or so. Brewers add so-called *dry hops* to beer that has already fermented to extract fresh hops aromatics. This practice is commonly observed in American IPAs and double IPAs, but virtually any style of beer can be successfully dry hopped. But more about that later.

OTHER BOIL ADDITIONS

Hops aren't the only thing we can add to boiling wort. In fact, anything that we'd like dissolved in our beer can go in. Other boil additions include the following:

- **Spices:** From anise and coriander to orange peel and spruce tips, there's no end to the botanical flavorings you can lend to your beers. Most spices are added in the last five minutes of the boil to preserve their delicate aromatic compounds.
- **Fruits:** Name any fruit you can think of, and there's a good chance it has found its way into a beer. Fruit may be added at various times during the brewing process, including the boil. If added to the boil, it's best added at the end.
- **Lactose:** Lactose is milk sugar, and brewer's yeast can't ferment it. Adding it to the boil in the last 10 minutes will slightly sweeten your homebrew. It's most commonly used for milk stouts.
- **Kettle finings:** Kettle finings, the most common of which include Irish moss (above middle) and Whirlfloc (above left), are products that enhance beer clarity. Add them in the final 10 minutes of the boil to promote clearer beer down the road.
- **Yeast nutrients:** Malt-based wort is an excellent source of nutrients for brewer's yeast, and it only makes sense: We've bred the yeast to thrive in it. However, wort that includes a large amount of unmalted adjuncts may benefit from a small addition of nutrients (above right). They're available at your homebrew retailer and are best added in the last 5 minutes of the boil.

COOLING AND COLD BREAK

When you kill the heat to your boil kettle, you officially enter what's known as the *cold side* of brewing. Up to and including the boil, you don't need to sanitize because the boil does it for you. The minute you remove heat, though, *everything* that touches your wort must be sanitized.

Immediately after the boil, we rapidly cool the wort from the boiling point down to the temperature at which we intend to ferment our beer, typically 60–70°F (16–21°C) for ales or 45–55°F (7–13°C) for lagers. Many brewers use an immersion wort chiller, which is a specialized piece of equipment that quickly cools wort.

If you don't have an immersion wort chiller, or if your brew kettle is too small to accommodate one, an ice bath is the next best thing. Just fill your kitchen sink or a large tub with cold tap water and ice cubes or cold gel packs. Cover your brew kettle when you shut off the heat to steam sanitize the lid and then place the whole thing in the ice bath, taking care that the water level doesn't rise too far and seep into your wort under the lid. Leave the brew pot in the cold bath for as long as is necessary to cool it to fermentation temperature.

No matter your cooling method, one thing you may or may not witness is the so-called *cold break*. Extract-based wort tends to produce less of this stuff than does wort freshly prepared from malted barley kernels, but it can show up in any beer. Cold break is the name for the

coagulated proteins that clump together and give your wort an appearance not unlike miso soup or egg drop soup (above left). It's fascinating to watch, and I always feel particularly accomplished when my wort produces a strong cold break. Truth be told, though, there's nothing inherently good or bad about it. It just is.

Some brewers like to allow the cold break to precipitate to the bottom of the boil kettle so that they can gingerly siphon ultra-clear wort from around it. You'll probably run across the term *whirlpooling* here and there, which just means stirring the wort vigorously (with a sanitized spoon) and then allowing it to settle: the cold break and other debris then naturally form a compact cone right in the middle of the bottom of the kettle, which makes it easy to leave all that stuff behind.

I rarely go to such lengths. In most cases, I just pour the cooled wort, cold break and all, right into the fermentor, through a sanitized strainer to keep hops material out. The cold break actually contains some nutrients that benefit yeast health, and if you ferment

in a clear container such as a carboy, it is a magical experience to watch the cold break proteins swirl around at the height of fermentation.

It's your call. If the cold break bothers you, then by all means, let it settle out. Otherwise, just accept it and move on: a little cold break isn't going to make or break your beer. You'll rack your beer off the cold break after fermentation anyway, so it's just a question of whether you get it out of the way now or later.

Checking Gravity

With your freshly prepared wort happily cooled down to room temperature or so, it's almost time to add yeast and start fermentation. But before you do, there's one piece of housekeeping that, like making the bed, is easy to forget when you're in a hurry. But it's a good habit to get into, and that's taking a *specific gravity reading*.

Specific gravity is an expression of how much dissolved sugar is available in wort for yeast to convert to alcohol and carbon dioxide. Your first specific gravity reading is the *original gravity*. As fermentation proceeds, the specific gravity (which is a ratio of a substance's density to that of water) progressively decreases until it bottoms out at *final gravity*, a measure of density of the finished beer.

Taking an original gravity reading tells you where your beer starts. It's a bit like taking a compass bearing to figure out where you are. Only by knowing where you start can you possibly hope to guess where you'll end up (my, that's philosophical!). Taking an original gravity reading is as simple as pulling a sample of wort using a thief (right) and plopping a hydrometer down into the sample. Let it settle and then read the liquid level off the scale printed on the side of the hydrometer. If you ferment in a bucket, you can even just float the sanitized hydrometer directly in the wort.

As fermentation progresses, you can take gravity readings along the way to see how far your beer has come. Let's consider a fairly basic American pale ale. A typical progression for specific gravity might go like this:

BREW DAY (BD): Original gravity 1.055
BD+1: Gravity reading 1.055
BD+2: Gravity reading 1.050
BD+3: Gravity reading 1.040
BD+4: Gravity reading 1.030
BD+5: Gravity reading 1.025
BD+6: Gravity reading 1.020
BD+7: Gravity reading 1.015
BD+8: Gravity reading 1.013
BD+9: Gravity reading 1.012
BD+10: Gravity reading 1.011
BD+11: Gravity reading 1.011
BD+12: Gravity reading 1.011

This progression is purely hypothetical, but it demonstrates how specific gravity falls as wort ferments into beer. And when that specific gravity finally settles at a stable number, in this case 1.011, we call that final number the final gravity. But only by knowing your initial, or original, gravity, can you reliably track the progress of your beer.

With a gravity reading in hand, you're ready to move on to the main event: fermentation, where wort becomes beer.

MOVING ON

Everything up to and including the boil is done in preparation for the moment to come: pitching yeast. With the boil behind us, we enter the cold side in earnest and must pay careful attention to sanitation. But our efforts will be rewarded with the best beer possible.

Chapter 8

Fermentation

Instinct must be thwarted just as one prunes the branches of a tree so that it will grow better. – Henri Matisse

YOU WILL VERY LIKELY GO mad during your first beer's *fermentation,* the fifth essential step in brewing beer. Don't feel bad if you do: It happens to all of us.

You will probably wonder whether you did something wrong if the airlock doesn't commence bubbling within a few hours of your having pitched yeast. Or you might open the lid after a week, find yourself horrified at the ring of goop lining the fermentor, and wonder if your beer has become infected.

There's a reason that Charlie Papazian, author of *The Complete Joy of Homebrewing*, instructs readers, "Relax. Don't worry. Have a homebrew (RDWHAHB)." All of your instincts are to become alarmed and anxious, but part of the journey that is homebrewing is heeding the advice of such legends as Papazian and Matisse.

Ignore your instincts. Resist the urge to obsess over your fermenting beer. There's virtually nothing you can do about it once fermentation starts anyway, aside from a few minor tweaks that may or may not do much. So try not to think about it.

But before you can *not* think about it, you need to add some yeast.

ADDING OXYGEN

Oxygen is a critical component of yeast health, but when we boil wort, oxygen is carried away on wafting water vapor. Thus, when preparing to add yeast to freshly boiled and cooled wort, it's a good idea to add oxygen back in.

The pros use inline systems that let them measure exactly how many parts per million (ppm) of pure oxygen they inject into wort as it passes from boil kettle to fermentor. Few homebrewers bother to go to quite that level of trouble, although many of us do use a pure oxygen supply to deliver oxygen by way of a stainless-steel diffusion stone.

Wyeast Laboratories has conducted research indicating that shaking your full fermentor for 40 seconds introduces about 8 ppm of dissolved oxygen (wyeastlab .com/hb_oxygenation.cfm/). That's a little shy of the recommended 10 ppm, but for most of us brewing average-strength ales, it works pretty well. If you get into high-gravity ales and moderate-to-high gravity lagers, then you might want to consider buying a 0.5-micron stone and an oxygen system. But when you're just starting out, you'll be fine if you just shake and splash as much as you can.

Note that dry yeast includes everything it needs to reproduce as part of the drying process, so you only need add oxygen to wort if using liquid yeast. But you won't hurt anything if you do oxygenate all of your wort, and sometimes I still oxygenate when using dry yeast just as a matter of habit. Once it becomes part of your brewday process, it just feels natural.

PITCHING YEAST

After wort has been oxygenated, it's time to *pitch*, or add, the yeast. There's nothing punctilious about this, but feel free to make it into a production if you like, especially if it's your first time. In Chapter 12, we discuss

Ale and Lager: Two Members of the Same Family

Veteran brewers sometimes avoid the ale-versus-lager conversation when talking to beginners, or they give it only passing mention, as if it's the zymurgical equivalent of sitting down with your parents for the birds-and-the-bees talk. "Yes, we'll talk about lager," they say. "But let's wait until you're old enough. Until then, here's an informative brochure."

Poppycock. If you can brew ale, you can brew lager. I would argue that for most homebrewers, brewing lager from extract is easier and more straightforward than brewing ale entirely from grain. The equipment requirements are modest, and you open up a whole family of beer styles that would otherwise be inaccessible. And yes, it's no secret that I am a little partial to lagers.

I'm not suggesting you *should* attempt a Czech-style Pilsner as your first homebrew. But if Czech-style Pilsner is your favorite style, and that's really what you want to brew, why not? My third homebrew was a Bavarian-style Helles (one of my favorite styles), and I rather enjoyed it. It wasn't the best beer I've ever brewed, but it certainly wasn't the worst.

Brewing ale and brewing lager are, indeed, different, but the differences are not as stark as you might think. Ales ferment at or near room temperature, while lagers ferment about 20°F (11°C) cooler than that. That's the big secret. Yes, lagers traditionally spend a few weeks at near-freezing temperatures after fermentation, but this practice improves ales as well. Time can heal many wounds, whether those wounds are inflicted at room temperature or in sweater weather.

All you really need to brew lager is a location that is somewhere in the range of 45-55°F (7-13°C) and a healthy population of lager yeast. Some brewers use a basement or garage in the winter. Others use a temperature-control device to override the internal thermostat of an old chest freezer or refrigerator. I've even used a room in my house that doesn't quite get enough heat.

If you do choose to ferment your wort with a lager strain of yeast instead of an ale strain (and that's really about all it takes), then just make sure to use twice as much yeast as you normally would and expect fermentation to take close to 2 weeks. If possible, try to increase the temperature of your fermenting lager around day 9 or 10 for a so-called *diacetyl rest*, which just revs up yeast metabolism a bit so the yeast cells clean up after themselves.

Once fermentation is over, transfer your lager to another vessel, such as a glass carboy, and allow it to rest at about 35°F (2°C) for at least 4 weeks. I usually count on 1 week for every 10 points of original gravity, so 4 weeks for 1.040, 6 weeks for 1.060, and so on. Then prime, bottle, and condition as you would any other beer.

Oh, and don't be surprised when your lager fermentation makes the room smell like sulfur. I fermented that first Helles in the garage, and my car smelled of rotten eggs for the better part of a week.

the mechanics of preparing the yeast or a yeast starter.

With yeast added, you simply close up your fermentor by closing the lid if it's a bucket or securing the stopper if it's a carboy and then attaching an airlock. Place your fermentor in a dark, cool spot where it's unlikely to see the light of day. If light is a potential issue and you're fermenting in a glass carboy, cover it with a towel or even a black trash bag to keep light from degrading the precious hops within.

TEMPERATURE CONTROL

Beginner brewers don't often consider temperature control until they want to brew up a lager (See "Ale and Lager: Two Members of the Same Family," at left), but temperature control is one of the most important things you can do to turn good wort into great beer, ale and lager alike.

For most ale strains, fermentation should take place at around 65–70°F (18–21°C). Generally speaking, it's a good idea to start fermentation on the low end of the range and let the fermentor gradually warm to the upper end of the range as it nears completion. In practice, this is hard to do without precise temperature control.

Beginner brewers will do just fine by selecting a reliably cool spot in the house. Basements, closets, pantries, and crawl spaces are all good candidates. If you have central heat and enough space, consider closing the vents to your guest bedroom and fermenting in there.

Eventually, you might consider repurposing an old refrigerator or freezer and overriding the internal thermostat with a special temperature controller that lets you specify the exact temperature you want. Basic controllers have become quite affordable in the last decade or so, and many higher-end models (like the one pictured below) even let you program in a custom temperature program that changes by the day, or even the hour if you want that level of detail.

LETTING IT GO

The most difficult part of fermentation is likely to be suppressing your natural inclination to check on things and verify that all is well. By all means, kneel down and sniff the airlock as it bubbles. Every homebrewer does this for every batch of beer.

But do leave your escapades at that. Once active fermentation is underway, there's very little you can do, and any action you choose to take is only likely to make things worse and cause you even more stress. So do as Charlie does, and RDWHAHB. Or at the very least have a great craft beer.

MOVING ON

Like adolescence, fermentation is a confusing time during which you may feel urges to act impulsively and irresponsibly. Try to settle down and enjoy the ride. Unlike adolescence, fermentation lasts just a week or two, after which time you can enjoy a drink without having to sneak it from your parents' liquor cabinet.

Chapter 9

Maturation

This suspense is terrible. I hope it will last.
– Gwendolen Fairfax in Oscar Wilde's The Importance of Being Earnest

WINE. CHEESE. DAME HELEN MIRREN. Some things just get better with age. And beer is no different, up to a point, anyway. All beer needs a period of time during which rough edges can smooth, flavors can meld, and yeast cells can clean up after themselves. *Maturation,* the sixth essential step in brewing beer, is as critical a phase as fermentation itself, and it can be as bearable as a couple of days or as insufferable as a couple of years.

For beginner and veteran brewers alike, waiting doesn't come naturally. You want to try your homebrew, and you want to try it *now.* Generally speaking, the stronger the beer, the longer you'll have to wait to taste it. Fortunately, most average ales need only a couple of weeks, which is one reason I advise beginners to brew something simple the first few times out.

I've found it helps to buy a 6-pack, 12-pack, case, or keg—whatever you need—of a commercial beer that's in the same style as the homebrew you're currently maturing. Each time you crack open that Sierra Nevada Pale Ale, Oskar Blues Old Chub, Bell's Two Hearted Ale, or Big Sky Moose Drool, you can close your eyes, take a long sip, and imagine what it will be like in a few days or weeks when you finally get to taste your own fermented wonder.

The maturation period is also the time to introduce additions such as dry hops, fruit, chiles, or oak. And once the waiting period is over, it's on to packaging, the final step in moving your homebrewed beer from grain to glass.

WHEN DOES FERMENTATION END AND MATURATION BEGIN?

The only way to know that your beer is ready for maturation is to measure the specific gravity, which is an indirect indicator of density, and thus, how much of the available sugar in the original wort has been consumed by the yeast. This number steadily drops during fermentation and eventually reaches a steady final gravity (FG). Typical final-gravity readings for a few styles are given in the table below.

After three gravity readings on consecutive days yield the same specific gravity at or near the expected final gravity, your beer has passed out of fermentation and into maturation. The maturation phase is known by many names, including conditioning and secondary fermentation. As I mention in the first chapter, I have no love for the term secondary fermentation because, usually, little to no fermentation occurs. I much prefer maturation or conditioning, which more precisely describes the purpose of this period.

WHEN IS FERMENTATION FINISHED?	
Beer Style	Typical Final Gravity
Light American lager	0.998–1.008
Irish stout	1.007–1.011
American IPA	1.010–1.018
American barleywine	1.016–1.030

TO RACK OR NOT TO RACK

Some brewing guides insist that you should move fresh beer to a secondary container, such as a 5-gallon (19-liter) carboy soon after fermentation subsides to get the beer away from the large cake of yeast that flocculates to the bottom. Growing numbers of modern homebrewers, however, eschew the secondary fermentor altogether and feel that some further contact with the yeast promotes a smoother, less rough product in the end.

This is one of those things you'll have to decide for yourself. I recommend trying both approaches and seeing which you prefer. My approach is not to rack anything that I intend to package within a month: These beers don't need much aging and can go straight from the fermentor to bottles or kegs. You can safely leave beer on top of the yeast for at least a month without risking off-flavors, so long as storage conditions remain relatively cool.

Although I've found that most beer can remain in contact with the yeast cake for well beyond a month, I usually rack anything that needs to undergo extended aging. This is as much about freeing up space in my fermentors as it is about removing it from trub, to be honest. But it is true that yeast eventually dies, and when it does, it can self-consume, or *autolyze*. Autolysis can lend some unfavorable flavors to your homebrew, including a soy sauce–like umami character that

can actually work in certain very dark styles. It is, in most cases, however, undesirable.

The table below compares some of the pros and cons of racking versus simply leaving your beer in the fermentor.

DRY HOPS, WOOD, AND OTHER ADDITIONS

You will almost definitely want to rack your beer to a secondary vessel if you want to make any additions during maturation. There's nothing stopping you from adding these sorts of things to the primary, but it's usually cleaner and more convenient to have a separate vessel for additions. Certainly anything you intend to age for months should be racked to a secondary.

Dry Hops

Dry hops are added after fermentation has finished, and they deliver that unmistakably fresh punch of hops aroma that defines today's hoppiest styles such as double IPA. Alcohol is an excellent solvent and effectively extracts precious hops oils. As it happens, carbon dioxide is also an excellent solvent, so dry hopping is one way to reintroduce aromas that may have been driven away during the turbulent fermentation process.

Add dry hops to fermented beer and remove after a week of contact. There's

virtually no benefit to leaving the hops longer, and you run the risk of introducing an inappropriate vegetal character. Some brewers simply dump dry hops right in, but I prefer to bundle them in a sanitized nylon mesh bag to make removal a cinch.

Note that because of their antimicrobial properties, there is no need to sanitize dry hops. Just add them to your fermented beer and get on with your life.

Wood

Wood aging, most commonly with oak, can impart some unique flavors to your homebrew, including

- **Vanilla**
- **Butterscotch**
- **Caramel**
- **Toffee**
- **Tannins**
- **Coconut**
- **Chocolate**
- **Coffee**

RACKING PROS AND CONS	
Leaving in primary fermentor	**Racking to a secondary vessel**
No extra steps	One extra step
Less opportunity for introducing oxygen	Potential to introduce oxygen
Potential for off-flavors if beer remains in contact with yeast for extended periods (months)	Reduced risk of yeast-related off-flavors
Potential to retain substantial sediment in final beer	May result in clearer beer
If the primary fermentor is plastic (which is somewhat permeable), extended age can introduce oxygen.	A glass or stainless secondary vessel is oxygen impermeable and more suitable for long-term storage than plastic.

Products such as wood chips, cubes, and spirals deliver the character of an oak barrel in a convenient, easy-to-handle package. Soaking those chips, cubes, and spirals in spirits or wine before adding them to your beer can introduce even more powerful flavors and aromas, such as the vanilla and butterscotch notes we expect from a bourbon barrel–aged stout.

Soak oak products in spirits for a week or two before adding them to your beer. The alcohol in the spirits will sanitize the oak. If, however, you don't want to introduce spirits character, consider boiling oak products for a few minutes to sanitize. This also removes some of the harsher tannic components that you may not want to include in your beer.

Fruit

As I mentioned before, it seems as if just about every possible type of fruit has found its way into beer at one point or another. Fruit flavors and aromas can be the star of the show, as they are in many American wheat beers, or they can subtly complement the hops and yeast-derived phenols of a Belgian ale. And what stout lover wouldn't enjoy the rich decadence of dark cherries in a Russian imperial stout?

When you add fruit to your maturing beer, some of the natural sugars may actually prompt a true second fermentation (in this case, the term *secondary fermentation* is completely appropriate) as the delicate fruity aromas and flavors are imparted. Fruit may be added as a fresh, frozen, or pureed product. Avoid fruit extracts, however, which often have a character reminiscent of cough syrup.

Fresh fruit should be frozen before use to sanitize it. Bagged frozen fruit and canned purees from the supermarket can be used directly from their packaging.

Chiles

You might automatically think of heat when you consider chiles, but the best chile beers feature a robust chile flavor, sometimes fiery, sometimes mild. Roasting chiles introduces an additional level of earthy complexity: If you've ever had a fresh green-chile beer in New Mexico, you know how addictive such examples can be.

Both fresh and dried chiles can be successfully added to beer. Introduce them about a week before packaging and then remove, but let your taste buds be your ultimate guide. As with fruit, it's best to freeze fresh chiles before adding to sanitize. Dried chiles may be soaked in a small amount of vodka and then added to the beer.

Chocolate

Chocolate adds wonderful complexity to beer and is especially at home in dark styles such as stout and porter. Cacao nibs are the most suitable type of chocolate to add to secondary because they contain little head-destroying fat. Soak them in a little vodka for a couple of days and then add to your beer.

Coffee

Coffee is a natural complement to porters and stouts, but it works surprisingly well in pale styles as well. Like hops, coffee offers bitterness, flavor, and, aroma. Most of the time, you're probably after the latter two, but in some cases coffee bitterness can lend balance to an otherwise too-sweet beer. Freshly brewed and cooled or cold-brewed coffee can be added straight to the secondary fermentor. Cracked (not finely ground) coffee beans can be used similarly but should be removed before packaging.

You'll come across various theories about the best way to add coffee and whether it should be sanitized. If using cracked coffee beans, soaking in vodka is an effective way to sanitize. I personally prefer to use straight espresso shots or a French press preparation that I whip up right before bottling. I'm willing to accept the very small risk of contamination in exchange for the incredibly rich coffee flavor that such methods produce. Keep in mind that the alcohol and hops in fermented beer make it much less vulnerable to infection than unfermented wort.

Spices

Spices are the non-leafy portions of plants and can include berries, seeds, roots, and bark. They should be as fresh as possible and freshly ground. A great tool to keep around is an inexpensive "whirlybird" type coffee grinder. Use it exclusively for your spices because coffee oils are hard to remove. Your spice options are almost limitless. Commonly used varieties include:

- Cardamom
- Caraway
- Chicory
- Cinnamon
- Cloves
- Coriander
- Ginger
- Grains of paradise
- Juniper berries
- Kaffir lime leaves
- Lavender
- Lemongrass
- Lemon verbena
- Licorice
- Nutmeg
- Peppercorns
- Peppermint
- Spearmint
- Star anise
- Woodruff
- Wormwood

As with other additions, you may choose to sanitize spices by soaking in a little vodka, or you can simply add them as they are.

MOVING ON

The conditioning phase is an important one. Not only does it give your beer time to mellow before packaging, but it's also an opportunity to infuse the beer with additional character from coffee, spices, fruit, oak, and other products. Once your beer has completed its maturations phase, it's time to package it. For many homebrewers, especially beginners, that means bottling.

Chapter 10

Packaging

A tavern is a place where madness is sold by the bottle. – Jonathan Swift

PACKAGING, THE SEVENTH ESSENTIAL STEP in brewing beer, is the key step that transports beer from your fermentor to your face. Without it, we'd all have to grab long straws, gather 'round the beer, and dig in. But thanks to bottles and kegs, you can serve your homebrew just like the pros.

Bottling and *kegging* are sometimes left as an afterthought. You'll run across innumerable recipes that go through meticulous detail on how to mash grain, add hops, and select just the right yeast strain. And almost all of them end with "then bottle or keg." Don't worry, we get into more details here.

BOTTLING

As a beginner, you'll probably bottle your homebrew, so that's what I focus on in this book. However, I provide some aspects of kegging in this chapter as an introduction to serving draft beer at home.

Types of Bottles

It is entirely possible to purchase brand-new, never-used beer bottles from a store, and there's nothing wrong with doing so. However, if you don't mind scraping a few labels, you can also get bottles from a liquor store that—this is key—come with beer in them. Drink the beer (ideally over a period of weeks—perhaps while your beer ferments and matures), clean the bottles, remove the labels, sanitize, and you're ready to go.

If you choose to reuse bottles, be sure to source only models with pry-off caps—which is to say, bottles that require an opener. Bottles that accept screw caps, while convenient for the backyard barbecue, aren't suitable for the kind of bottle capping we do at home.

The most common beer bottles you're likely to encounter include the following:

- **Longnecks:** These are the most common and most familiar beer bottles you'll run across. American longnecks hold an even 12 fluid ounces (355 ml), while those from Europe and other metric civilizations hold 330 ml (11.2 fl oz). These are the preferred type of bottle for most homebrewers. You'll need about fifty of these to package 5 gallons (19 l) of homebrew.

- **Bombers:** Probably the second-most-common bottle among homebrewers, bombers hold 22 fluid ounces (651 ml), which means that for every eleven standard longnecks, you need only six bombers (i.e., about thirty to package 5 gallons (19 l) of homebrew). Fewer bottles to fill means less time bottling and more time brewing! Cap a bomber just as you would a standard longneck.

- **Shortnecks and stubbies:** A few commercial breweries package in squatty bottles. Sierra Nevada Brewing Company and Alaskan Brewing Company, for example, use bottles that are slightly wider than the standard-issue longneck and feature a somewhat shorter neck. Stubbies are those favored by Redhook, Red Stripe, and Full Sail's Session series. Some brewers use these kinds of bottles, but for every success story, there seems to be another involving improper seals or broken glass. Use them if you can, but don't feel bad if you can't.

■ **European half liters:** These bottles are great if you can find them. At 500 ml each (16.9 fl oz), their capacity is much closer to a true U.S. pint than the standard longneck. Furthermore, they tend to be made from thicker glass, which makes them sturdier and less likely to explode if you accidentally overcarbonate. I also happen to think they look nicer than most beer bottles. You'll need about forty of these to package 5 gallons (19 l) of homebrew.

■ **Swing-top "Grolsch" style bottles:** Swing-top bottles are a dream to use. No bottle capper is needed; just fill the bottle and clamp down the integrated stopper using the wire bale. The gaskets need to be changed from time to time, but that's about the only disadvantage to these trusty beer holders. Like European half liters, these are usually sturdier and can handle somewhat greater pressure than standard-issue bottles.

■ **Champagne bottles:** Champagne bottles offer perhaps the most elegant presentation for your homebrew, but they may or may not be the right solution for you. Corking these bottles requires a completely different set of equipment. Most champagne bottles accept crown caps, but you'll need different-sized caps for European and North American bottles, as well as a bench capper, which is a sturdy device that can cap just about anything. I love using these kinds of bottles, but I recommend waiting until you're well into homebrewing before trying them on for size. A major advantage of champagne bottles is that they are heavy and stand up to much higher pressures than single-use beer bottles.

■ **Belgian bottles:** Belgian bottles are incredibly beautiful, but most of them need to be corked. A few will accept bottle caps, but again, a bench capper is the preferred device with which to seal them.

Nonetheless, if you've been steadily building up a sizeable supply of beer bottles from the local order of Trappists, it might be worth looking into the equipment you need to seal these beauties.

Racking and Priming

Once you have your selected arsenal of bottles, you need to prepare your beer for the bottling process. Homebrewers use a method called *bottle conditioning* to create carbon dioxide within the bottle; this method involves adding a small amount of sugar to each bottle before filling it with beer and then sealing the cap.

Over a period of several days, residual yeast that remains in the unfiltered beer (there's yeast in there even if you can't see it) consumes that sugar, producing carbon dioxide and a small amount of alcohol in the process. This carbon dioxide, trapped within the bottle, is absorbed into the beer and creates natural effervescence.

It's entirely possible to individually dose each bottle with sugar, but doing so is tedious, boring, and unnecessary. Instead, we do what is called *bulk priming*, in which we mix a liquid sugar solution right into the whole batch before we bottle it. This is most effectively executed using a bottling bucket.

A bottling bucket is just a regular bucket that has a spigot in the bottom. Finished matured beer is racked into this bucket **(1,2)**, and as the beer flows in, we pour in a carefully measured solution of sugar **(3)**. The natural swirling that occurs during the transfer process is sufficient to thoroughly mix the sugar throughout the finished beer, and when racking is complete, we have a mixture of beer and sugar that's ready for bottling and carbonation.

Filling and Capping

With our bucket full of primed beer **(4)**, it's time to fill each bottle and snap on a cap. Filling is done right from the bottling bucket by connecting a special *bottling wand* to the integrated spigot using a length of plastic tubing. The bottling wand **(5)** has a tip that permits beer to flow when pressed against the bottom of a bottle and halts said flow when withdrawn. Thus, we can fill each bottle individually with our mixture of beer and sugar.

You could cap each bottle immediately after filling it, but most of us find that an assembly line setup speeds things along considerably. I usually fill twelve bottles in a row and then cap those twelve and put them away before moving on to the next set in the series. Why twelve? Well they fit in a 12-pack holder. You might go with six or twenty-four or the whole batch. It's your call.

Capping the bottles requires a bottle capper, which for most beginners will be a wing-style capper. Simply place a sanitized crown cap on top of a bottle and place the capper's bell over the crown. Pushing down on the two wings engages a pair of metal plates that grasp the bottle's neck on either side while simultaneously plunging the bell down and onto the cap. When the two wings snap down to become horizontal and parallel to the bottling surface, the cap seats firmly onto the bottle, and you're done **(6)**. Easy peasy.

Repeat for the duration of your batch and then clean up your mess. Once you get the hang of it, you can package fifty bottles or so in less than an hour. If you have a dishwasher, the bottom rack is a convenient place to hold bottles as you fill them. When your task is complete, just close the door to contain the inevitable spilled beer.

Bottle Conditioning

Because bottled homebrew relies on the natural activity of yeast to create carbonation, you need to give those yeast cells the best environment to do their thing. And that means a room-temperature—or slightly warmer—location, ideally one in the dark. Some Belgian brewers even maintain special "warm rooms" in which bottled beer can condition and carbonate. (Some beginning lager brewers wonder whether lagers need to be held at cold temperatures during this phase, and the answer is no. You can carbonate your bottles of lager at room temperature or higher without having any flavor impact on the final product.)

It will take at least 2 weeks for your beer to carbonate. I recommend waiting 3 weeks if you can, but I realize this is hard to do. Keep in mind, though, that the following characteristics serve to prolong the amount of time it takes for beer to carbonate and condition:

- **Strength** >>The stronger the beer, the more slowly it carbonates.
- **Age** >>A beer that has been aging for 6 months will take longer to carbonate than one that is only a week or two old. There's simply less yeast to do the job.
- **Temperature** >> The colder the storage environment, the longer carbonation takes.
- **Lager** >> By virtue of the long cold lagering phase that characterizes these beer styles, many emerge from the lagering chamber with fewer yeast cells in suspension than an equivalent ale. There's still yeast in there, but relying on it may mean that your bottles take several weeks to condition.

If you're worried that your beer may experience difficulty with carbonation due to one of these factors, feel free to sprinkle a sachet of dry champagne yeast into the bottling bucket as you rack your beer. A little extra yeast may just be the boost your beer needs to condition more quickly. (Consider storing your bottled beer in sturdy boxes or plastic tubs.)

Remember: Two weeks at least!

KEGGING

I think that every homebrewer dreams of serving beer on draft in the comfort of his or her own home, and an entire sector of homebrewing revolves around enabling you to do just that. This isn't a book about kegging, but it is worth taking some time to introduce you to the practice so that you have basic familiarity with the idea. If you decide that kegging is right for you, check out Craft Beer & Brewing's online courses (available at learn.beerandbrewing.com):

- **Kegging Your Beer** introduces you to the kegs themselves and shows you how to disassemble and put them back together for maintenance. You also learn how to sanitize and fill kegs, determine an appropriate serving pressure, and more.
- **Draft Systems** goes beyond basic kegging to teach you how to build and maintain a draft-beer serving system, commonly called a kegerator. In this course, you learn how to build an entire draft system from the ground up and even how to work with nitrogen for a creamy Guinness-style stout.

Types of Kegs

You may be familiar with commercial kegs, also known as Sankey kegs. These are the industry-standard stainless-steel vessels available in half-barrel (15.5 gallon), quarter-barrel (7.75 gallon), and sixth-barrel (5.16 gallon) sizes. The sizes are different, but all use the same single-piece coupler, which is commonly called a tap. The coupler admits pressurized carbon dioxide into the keg and allows beer to flow out of the keg, through a beverage line, out of a faucet, and into your glass.

If you've ever been at a party where kegs of beer are available in large buckets of ice, chances are the couplers didn't connect to carbon dioxide tanks. More likely, there was a hand pump that you'd use to pressurize the keg and force beer out through the cobra-shaped picnic faucet. These are only to be used in situations where the keg will be emptied within a brief period of time. Air causes beer to go stale, so professional and home draft systems always rely upon carbon dioxide, not air, to dispense beer.

Homebrewers rarely use Sankey kegs. Most of us use old soda kegs, which conveniently hold exactly 5 gallons (19 l) and feature a large, oval-shaped lid that is easily removed for racking beer right into the keg. Two posts on top of the keg accept carbon dioxide (the gas post) and provide an escape route for beer (the liquid post). These kegs are often called "Corny" kegs, which is short for Cornelius, one of the manufacturers that originally supplied these types of kegs to the soda industry.

Most soda manufacturers have switched to syrup-in-a-bag dispensing systems, in which syrup concentrates are mixed with carbonated water at the point of sale. For some time, this meant that legions of old soda kegs were

COMPONENT
MODEL NO. : K10C9(2)
I14AFC04E
Max Capacity : 2.5 Gallons
IIL Made in India
866-249-8196
PART#(CK1-N2.5-DRH-INX)
IMPORTED BY AMCYL, LTD.
--WARNING--
NEVER EXCEED MAXIMUM
WORKING PRESSURE of 130 P.S.I

bags of dry hops right in the keg. One retailer even sells a keg that can expand and collapse to accommodate different batch sizes, and another sells a 2.5-gallon (9.5 l) mini keg **(left)** that's built to easily fit inside a refrigerator.

Filling and Carbonating

There is neither mystery nor magic when it comes to getting your beer into a keg. Just rack beer right into it just as you'd rack into a secondary vessel for conditioning or a bottling bucket for bottling. You can even include priming sugar so that the beer carbonates in the keg, as if it were a large bottle. Due to physical laws that are beyond the scope of this book, only about a third as much priming sugar is needed, however—about 1.5 ounces (43 g) for 5 gallons (19 l) of beer.

Most brewers who package in kegs don't use priming sugar. Instead, we turn to the very same carbon dioxide that we later use to push beer out of the keg and into our glass. Carbon dioxide naturally dissolves into beer when applied at the right temperature and pressure. So, instead of priming the keg with sugar, many of us go ahead and place the keg in cold storage and hook up the gas, usually at around 12 to 15 pounds per square inch (83–103 kPa). Over the course of a week or so, that carbon dioxide dissolves into the beer and carbonates it right up. With a little shaking here and there, you can enjoy carbonated beer in as little as a day.

Getting beer into kegs is easy. Getting it out, however, requires a little extra effort.

Dispensing

In addition to a keg, you need, at the very least the following items:

- A **carbon dioxide cylinder (1)** (tank) filled with CO_2
- A **carbon dioxide regulator (2)** that attaches to

available at very attractive prices. Those days are drawing to a close as homebrewing grows in popularity and homebrewers like us snap up old soda kegs that may not look pretty but still hold pressure.

Fortunately, manufacturers have responded to the demand for quality kegs, and now purpose-built models are popping up everywhere. Some are merely replicas of what the soda companies once used, but modern interpretations may have such handy features as integrated pressure gauges and hooks for hanging

the cylinder and safely drops the gas pressure to what is needed for dispensing beer

- A length of **gas line (3)** and a **gas disconnect (4)** to connect the regulator to the keg
- A length of **beverage line (5)** and a **liquid disconnect (6)** to get beer out of the keg
- A **faucet (7)** that connects to the free end of the beverage line and delivers beer to your glass

In the simplest setups, all of the above simply sit in a refrigerator. When you want a beer, you open the door and use the same kind of picnic faucet you remember from parties to dispense beer. However, for many brewers, the appeal and convenience of a full home draft system are too alluring to ignore.

This means installing permanent, dedicated faucets just like those used to pour beer in your favorite craft-beer bar. Some of us use an old refrigerator and mount faucets right on the door. Others attach a shiny draft tower to the top of a small dorm-style refrigerator and mount faucets there. No matter how you do it, a home draft system is the ultimate way to serve and enjoy beer at home and a guaranteed way to reconnect with friends you never knew you had.

Homebrewing stores sell everything you could possibly need to keg your beer and maintain a clean, efficient draft system. We can't cover all of the details of kegging and serving draft beer in this book, but the online classes I mention on page 75 will teach you everything you need to know should you decide that route is for you.

MOVING ON

With our homebrew safely bottled or kegged, we have almost reached the final step of our journey: Serving and enjoying. Whether you bottle or keg your beer, there will be some period of waiting before you can finally pour a glass and enjoy the fruits of your labor. So be patient. Your reward is just around the corner.

Chapter 11

Serving Your Beer

The sense of smell, like a faithful counsellor, foretells its character.
– Jean Anthelme Brillat-Savarin,
The Physiology of Taste: Or, Transcendental Gastronomy

THIS CHAPTER MAY BE BRIEF, but it is—in many ways—the most important of them all; everything you have done until now has been in service of this very moment. Every malt, hops, yeast cell, and hour, and every piece of advice have been there to get you here.

This is when you taste your beer. And unlike tasting any other beer in the world, you can use what you taste now to affect how it could taste in the future.

GLASSWARE

This is not a book about glassware, but if you always gravitate to that conical frustum we call the Shaker glass (or Shaker pint), consider affording your choice a little more thought. After all, there's a reason that certain beer styles have come to be associated with certain glasses. Some glasses really do add to, complement, and improve the experience.

Chances are you already own a number of Shaker glasses. Spend enough time visiting breweries, and you're bound to come home with a few. Here are a few others to look out for.

- **Nonic pint glasses (1)** are the norm in English pubs and feature a slight bulge in the glass near the top to make them more stackable. Most hold an imperial pint, or about 19 fluid ounces (and many have a fill line to prove it). The classic glass for bitter, pale ale, brown ale, porter, and stout, this is my favorite beer glass for classic English styles and their American descendants.
- **Pilsner glasses (2)** are obviously well suited to Pilsner, but they work well with lagers of all types. Pilsner glasses are tall and narrow, with straight, sloping sides and a sturdy flat base.
- **IPA glasses (3)** are designed to release and concentrate hops aromas. The narrower base provides a convenient grip and a strategically designed surface for generating more head and releasing more hops aroma as you pour.
- **Tulip glasses (4)** have become almost ubiquitous among craft brewers, although their popularity is far greater than it perhaps ought to be. These are great for most Belgian styles, as well as for imperial IPA, imperial stout, barleywine, and a wide range of sour beers. I think the tulip is the new Shaker: ubiquitous but not necessarily the best one-size-fits-all vessel.
- The relatively new **Teku (5)** glass may look comical at first, but it's well suited to a broad range of styles. I particularly like it for sour ales, imperial stout, and Scotch ale.
- **Snifters** are reserved for the strongest of beers such as barleywine, imperial stout, and Belgian strong ales. The wide bowl is perfect for cupping in one hand, which warms the beer and enhances the sensory experience.
- **Stange** glasses are not very common in North America, but these diminutive 200 ml (6.8 fl oz) cylinders are the traditional delivery devices for Kölsch. They're also well suited to Altbier and smaller pours of most German lagers.
- The **Willibecher** is my favorite all-purpose glass for standard-strength ales and lagers of all geographical origins. The 500 ml (16.9 fl oz) Willibecher holds a generous measure and maintains a good head of foam from the first sip to the last. If I could keep only one glass in my collection, it would be this one.
- **Weissbier** glasses show off the fluffy white head of a well-brewed German Hefeweizen and accentuate the complex banana and clove notes so intimately tied to the style. They're without a doubt the sexiest beer glasses out there.
- **Dimpled mugs** are wonderfully frumpy and just the thing for serving a wide range of German and English styles. When you just want to drink some beer without thinking about it too hard, the dimpled mug is there for you. It's a classic for a reason.
- The 1-liter (33.8 fl oz) **Masskrug,** sometimes called a stein in North America, is the only acceptable vessel for drinking German lager at Oktoberfest.

BEER SERVING TEMPERATURE

Beer style	Serving temperature
American macro lager	As cold as possible
Light lager, blonde ale, most abbey-style Belgian ales	40–45°F (4–7°C)
Dark lager, American pale ale, American IPA, Weißbier, most sour ales	45–50°F (7–10°C)
English bitter, English IPA, brown ale, porter, stout, imperial stout, Doppelbock	50–55°F (10–13°C)

SERVING TEMPERATURE

The standard serving temperature for draft beer in the United States is 38°F (3°C), which is just right for mass-produced lager and much too cold for everything else. Generally speaking, the stronger and darker the beer, the warmer it should be served. The table on the previous page shows some rough guidelines, from coldest to coolest.

Naturally, your personal preference trumps anything you'll find in a chart. If you like your Pilsners at room temperature and your imperial stouts ice cold, be my guest! The point is to make serving temperature a conscious choice and not simply a by-product of whatever your refrigerator happens to be set at.

POURING YOUR BEER

Pouring a glass of homebrew is the same as pouring a glass of commercial beer. Tilt the glass at about 45° and pour beer until the glass is about two-thirds full. Then hold the glass vertically and fill it the rest of the way. This goes for both bottled and kegged beer.

If you're pouring from a bottle of homebrew, take care to leave the last few drops in the bottle. There's a small amount of yeast in homebrewed beer that usually settles to the bottom. Unless you're pouring Hefeweizen (in which case dump it all in!), try to leave that sediment in the bottle.

SENSORY ANALYSIS

Sensory evaluation is a crucial step in understanding how the decisions you made along the way translate into what you observe in the final glass. I recommend maintaining a journal—it need not be fancy—in which you can jot down your thoughts as you sample each batch of beer you make. Ideally, keep your impressions in the same place you write down your recipes so that you can make intelligent changes to your formulations.

- **Appearance:** Is the beer clear or cloudy? What color is it? What do you see in the glass? Is there a thick layer of persistent foam, or does the head die immediately? As you drink the beer, does lacing stick to the sides of the glass?
- **Aroma:** Swirl your beer gently in the glass and give it a good sniff. What do you smell? Grainy malt sweetness? Toast? Biscuits? What about hops? You might pick up pine, grapefruit, passion fruit, or even garlic. Yeast-derived esters may come across as fruit, while phenolics could come through as pepper, cloves, or smoke.
- **Flavor:** What do you taste? How do the flavor components parallel the aroma? How do they depart from it? How does the flavor change as the beer warms? Where do you notice the bitterness on your tongue, and how long does it last?
- **Mouthfeel:** How does the beer feel in your mouth? Is it smooth, crisp, warming, carbonic, or flabby? Do you notice lingering alcoholic warmth after the beer goes down?
- **Overall impression:** What do you think of the beer overall? What do you like about it? Do you enjoy drinking it? Would you make it again, and if so, what would you change about it? What might you keep the same?

You don't need to make this too complex. Just make some observations. Let your impressions guide your next brew day. The more you can identify what you experience with all five senses, the better equipped you'll be at designing your next beer. A flavor wheel (at right) is a great way to build a vocabulary of tasting terms that can help you organize your thoughts.

MOVING ON

Congratulations! You've followed each of the eight phases of brewing beer, just like the pros do it. But these past few chapters have been more about explaining the *why*. In the next chapter, we'll put it all together and walk you through all the *hows* of brewing and serving your own beer.

Beer Flavor Wheel

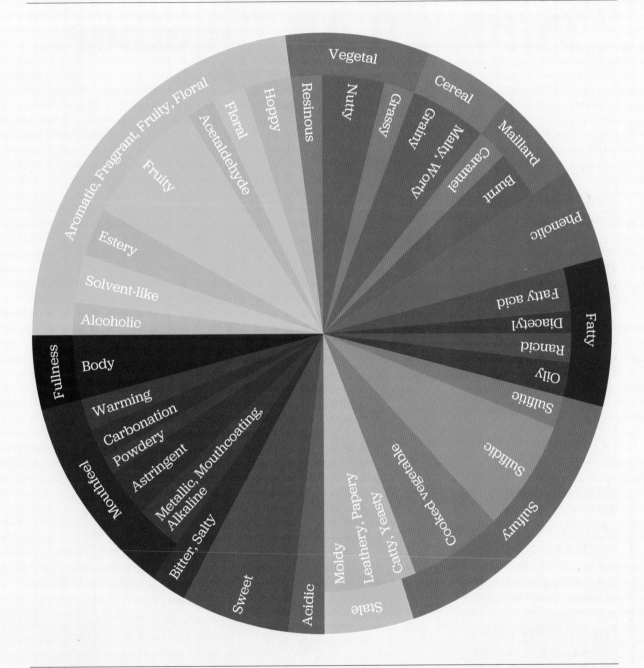

Adapted from beerflavorwheel.com, which was adapted from the flavor wheel originally developed by M. C. Meilgaard, C. E. Dalgliesh, and J. F. Clapperton in 1979

Chapter 12

Putting it All Together

For the great doesn't happen through impulse alone, and is a succession of little things that are brought together.
– Vincent van Gogh, in a letter to his brother, Theo, dated October 22, 1882

WE'VE COVERED A LOT OF ground, a succession of little things. But now the time has come to bring them together to make something truly unique and truly great: your very own homebrew.

This chapter is intentionally short on *why* and long on *how*. The goal isn't to theorize and explain: That's what previous chapters are for. Instead, the aim is to apply the science you've learned to the art of brewing beer. This chapter is about practice, not principles.

In each of the following sections, I describe exactly what equipment and ingredients you need before, during, and after brew day. For your convenience, lists of what you'll need to make beer from start to finish are provided in "Everything You Need to Get Started" (page 83). Once you have all of your equipment and consumables in place, it's time to start making beer!

PREPARATION FOR BREW DAY

In preparation for brew day, you really need only two things: creativity and—this is important—a beer recipe. The countdown to brew day is your opportunity to ensure you have everything you need to make great beer. It's a time for planning your brew and preparing your ingredients and equipment.

Planning Your Brew

A few days, weeks, or months before you want to brew, think about what you'd like to make. Maybe you already have a recipe kit. Or maybe you just know it's time to make beer, but you're not sure what you want. This is a time to ponder what you're in the mood for, or, if you want to have beer ready for a party or a holiday, how early you need to start to meet that goal. In general, plan on this time line:

- **1 week** to brew and ferment an average-strength **ale.**
- An additional **2-3 weeks** to mature an average-strength **ale.**
- **2 weeks** to brew and ferment an average-strength **lager.**
- An additional **4-6 weeks** to condition an average-strength lager.
- A final **2-3 weeks** to bottle condition and carbonate an average-strength **ale or lager.**

If you do the math, an average-strength ale takes about 6 weeks, start to finish. An average-strength lager needs about 10 weeks. These are merely averages, of course. Low-gravity ales (English mild and bitter, German Hefeweizen, American session IPA) take the least amount of time, while high-gravity ales and lagers (imperial stout, barleywine, Belgian dark strong ale, Doppelbock) take the longest.

It's not a bad idea to get out your calendar and pencil in the dates that you expect to brew, rack, and bottle. If travel plans, house guests, or social engagements are in your future, a calendar can help you plan your beer so

Everything You Need to Get Started

Hardware

Below is a list of the minimum hardware you need to brew, bottle, and carbonate a good batch of homebrew. You could get by with less, but you won't have nearly as much fun. You can find all of this (and much, much more) at any good homebrew retailer.

- Boil kettle or large stockpot, 3 gallons (12 l) or larger, with lid
- Large metal or plastic spoon
- Nylon mesh bag for steeping specialty grains (a muslin bag is also fine, but it's not reusable)
- Mesh colander
- 16-ounce (500 ml) glass measuring cup (if you are using dry yeast)
- 6.5-gallon (25 l) fermentation bucket with lid
- 6.5-gallon (25 l) bottling bucket with integrated spigot
- Wine thief
- Hydrometer
- Thermometer
- Airlock
- Auto-siphon
- 5 feet (1.5 m) or more of siphon tubing, preferably with a pinch clamp
- Bottling wand
- Fifty or more 12-ounce (355 ml) glass beer bottles (see pages 70–71 for quantities of bombers and European half liters)
- Fifty or more bottle caps (often called crown caps)
- Bottle capper
- Small saucepan

Ingredients and Consumables

If you purchase a prepackaged beer-recipe kit, then there's no need to buy ingredients separately, except, perhaps, yeast. Some kits don't include yeast, presumably for the same reasons that toys don't include batteries and cars don't come with floor mats. Moral: Check before you buy and purchase yeast if it's not part of the deal.

- Specialty grains, milled
- Malt extract, liquid or dry
- Hops, whole or pellets
- Yeast, liquid or dry
- A brewery-safe cleaner such as PBW or OxiClean
- Sanitizer of your choice, preferably Star San or Iodophor
- 4–5 ounces (113–142 g) corn sugar

Optional Equipment and Ingredients

Strictly speaking, you don't need any of the following to brew beer. However, you may want to procure these sooner rather than later because you'll almost certainly want them at some point.

- 2-liter Erlenmeyer flask or 64-ounce (1.9 l) growler jug, if you plan to propagate a yeast starter
- Extra dry malt extract (DME) for making a yeast starter
- Plastic funnel for transferring starter wort to your flask or growler jug

- Wort chiller
- 5-gallon (19 l) carboy with bung and airlock, if you want to mature your beer in a secondary vessel

Mandatory Items and Abstractions

You'll never brew a drop of (good) beer without these.

- Creativity
- A beer recipe
- Patience
- A cool, dark, quiet spot to stash your fermenting beer

How to Make a Yeast Starter

To propagate yeast from a packet of liquid yeast, you'll need the following:

- Sanitizer of your choice
- Dry malt extract (DME)
- Saucepan of at least 4 quarts (4 l) capacity, with lid
- Aluminum foil
- Thermometer
- Plastic funnel
- Erlenmeyer flask or 64-ounce (1.9 l) growler jug
- A packet of liquid yeast

Most homebrewers make yeast starters by the liter rather than by the quart because the math is much easier. Simply take your starter volume, in milliliters, and divide by 10 to obtain the number of grams of dried malt extract (DME) you need. That ratio yields a starter wort with an original gravity (OG) of about 1.035–1.040, which is ideal for growing yeast.

So, if you want to make a 1-liter starter, that's 1,000 milliliters. Divide by 10 to get 100, which means you'll add 100 grams of DME to your 1-liter starter.

Once you know how much water and DME you need, here's how to make your starter.

- Sanitize a flask (or growler jug), plastic funnel, a small sheet of aluminum foil, and thermometer. (If you use a borosilicate Erlenmeyer flask, you can boil in it right on a gas range—not electric, though—saving you the

step of sanitizing and the need for a funnel.)

- Prepare starter wort by combining the DME and water in your saucepan. A whisk can help break up the DME, which tends to form unwieldy clumps as soon as it hits water.
- Bring the DME and water to a boil, uncovered, and boil for 10 minutes. Watch for boilovers!
- After killing the heat, immediately cover the saucepan. Leave it for a minute or two to steam sanitize the lid and then place the covered saucepan in an ice-and-water bath, taking care not to allow water to seep in under the lid.
- Occasionally swirl the saucepan to aid cooling and use a sanitized thermometer to check the temperature once it is cool to the touch.
- When the starter wort temperature drops below 68°F (20°C), remove the saucepan from the ice bath and carefully pour the wort through a sanitized funnel into your flask or growler jug.
- Add your yeast to the starter wort through the sanitized funnel, then wrap sanitized foil loosely over the mouth of the vessel and leave it on the kitchen counter.

Give your starter a gentle swirl from time to time, every couple of hours or as convenient, for the next 2 to 3 days. You'll notice that the wort becomes opaque and a head of

foam may appear on top. You may also observe bubbles rising up as the yeast reproduces and ferments.

When fermentation is complete, activity will slow, the liquid will begin to clear, and a layer of yeast will settle to the bottom of the vessel. Place the whole thing in the refrigerator and let it wait for brew day. By the time you're ready to use it, the yeast will have dropped to the bottom and formed a nice compact layer. When you're ready to use the starter, decant most of the liquid, then swirl vigorously to re-suspend the yeast in the remaining liquid and pour the mixture into fresh wort.

A yeast starter will remain viable for at least a couple of weeks after you prepare it, but always give it a sniff before use. If it smells bad, don't use it!

that you don't miss dry-hop additions, temperature adjustments, and so on. If it's a big beer or a lager, you can also use a calendar to work backward from the day you want the beer to be ready and plan the brew accordingly.

When you know what you want to brew, head down to the homebrew store or visit your favorite online retailer and procure the ingredients you need, along with any special equipment you might not already have. (If you order online, keep in mind that many retailers now offer flat-rate or free shipping on orders above a certain size. Take time to play around with your shopping cart and shipping options if you order anything large or bulky, such as carboys, sacks of grain, kettles, and so on. I once managed to have a 55-pound (25 kg) sack of grain delivered right to my door for a mere $2.00 in additional shipping fees because my order included a carboy. Shipped on its own or with smaller items, that bag of grain would have incurred more than $25.00 in freight fees!)

Preparing Your Ingredients

When you brew from extract, there's little you need to do to prepare ingredients ahead of time, aside from ensuring that you have them. Store hops in the freezer until you need them, and keep malt extract and specialty grains in a cool, dry, dark location. The refrigerator is fine, but be sure to remove liquid malt extract a day or so in advance so that it will less begrudgingly pour come brew day.

If you intend to ferment your beer using one or more yeast packets pitched directly into the wort, just make sure you have your yeast and keep it in the refrigerator until brew day. However, if you plan to build up a large quantity of yeast cells from a smaller colony, you need to make a starter in advance so it's ready for brew day. I typically like to do this about 4 days before I plan to brew.

Making a starter is simple once you figure out how big it needs to be. There are some excellent Internet-based calculators to help you do this if you want to really dial in how much yeast you need. Just run a Google search for "yeast starter calculator." The ones at brewersfriend.com, mrmalty.com, and yeastcalculator.com were among the best at press time, but it wouldn't be surprising if others become available by the time you read this. It's a science that changes more than you might guess.

If you don't want to get too bogged down in the details, though, the rules of thumb in the table below are pretty good, *provided your yeast is fresh*. The numbers are based on suggested pitch rates on the Wyeast Laboratories website.

I don't claim that these are optimal for all situations, only that they're convenient guidelines that should get you close if you don't want to bother with lots of complexity. And it's crucial that your yeast be fresh, so try to buy it just a day or two before brew day if you can, and get it straight to your refrigerator until you need it.

If you have decided you need a starter and have calculated how big it needs to be, the process of making one

YEAST PITCH AMOUNTS

Original gravity (ale)	Original gravity (lager)	Yeast packets		Yeast starter
Less than 1.060	N/A	1		None
1.060–1.075	Less than 1.060	2	OR	1 liter
More than 1.075	1.060–1.075	3		2 liter
N/A	More than 1.075	4		3 liter

is straightforward. See "How to Make a Yeast Starter" (page 84) for complete step-by-step instructions. But remember, if you don't want to bother, you always have the option of buying a second or third packet of yeast.

BREW DAY

A typical brew day takes about 3 hours, including clean-up. For your brew day, you need the following items:

- **Sanitizer** of your choice, preferably Star San or Iodophor
- **Boil kettle** or large stockpot, 3 gallons (12 l) or larger, with lid
- Large metal or plastic **spoon**
- Mesh **colander**
- 16-ounce (500 ml) glass **measuring cup** (if you are using dry yeast)
- **Scissors** (for liquid yeast pouches or dry yeast)
- 6.5-gallon (25 l) **fermentation bucket** with lid
- **Thermometer**
- **Hydrometer**
- **Wine thief**
- **Airlock**
- Milled **specialty grains**
- Nylon **mesh bag** for steeping specialty grains (a muslin bag is fine, but it's not reusable)
- **Malt extract,** liquid or dry
- **Hops,** whole or pellets
- **Yeast** or yeast starter that you prepared earlier (if you're using one)
- A **brewery-safe cleaner** such as PBW or Oxi-Clean for cleanup

Brew day is the main event. This is when you prepare the wort that your yeast will ferment into beer. Your job on brew day boils down (ha!) to the following eight tasks:

- **Sanitizing** your equipment
- **Steeping specialty grains** in hot water
- **Adding malt extract** to the resulting grain water to make wort
- **Boiling wort** with hops
- **Cooling hot wort** to fermentation temperature
- **Transferring chilled wort** to a sanitized fermentor
- **Pitching yeast**
- **Cleaning up**

In the following sections, we cover how to do it, step by step. But before you start, if you are using packets of liquid yeast instead of a yeast starter, it's time to take the yeast out of the refrigerator (see "How to Use Liquid Yeast," page 88).

Sanitizing your Equipment

Truth be told, I usually sanitize my gear once the boil is underway to save time, but when you're first getting started, it's a good idea to go ahead and do it up front. That way you won't find yourself sans sanitized stuff when you need it. Here are the pieces you should most definitely sanitize:

- **Fermentation bucket and lid**
- **The lid to your brew pot**
- **Mesh colander**
- **16-ounce (500 ml) glass measuring cup** (if you are using dry yeast)
- **Scissors** (for liquid yeast pouches or dry yeast)
- **Thermometer**
- **Wine thief**
- **Hydrometer**
- **Airlock**

I like to prepare my sanitizer right in the fermentation bucket and drop everything else in there to soak while I complete other tasks. Remember, you don't need to sanitize your brew kettle or anything else that comes in contact with the wort before the end of the boil. But once the boil is over and done, only sanitized equipment should be used.

1 2
3 4

How to Use Liquid Yeast

1. If you are using an Activator product from Wyeast Laboratories, remove the packet from the refrigerator on brew day a couple of hours before you start brewing. Smack the pouch firmly with the palm of your hand as indicated on the instructions to rupture the internal nutrient pouch. Give the package a good shake and let it rest at room temperature until you're ready to pitch. The pouch will likely swell as the yeast cells within devour the nutrients.

2. If you are using a White Labs PurePitch product, simply remove the pouch from the refrigerator and leave it at room temperature until you need it. (At press time, White Labs was in the process of converting all of its yeast products to the new PurePitch packaging, but some strains were still sold in the older "test tube" vials. If you use one of the vials, or a product from East Coast Yeast, I recommend that you remove it from the refrigerator and twist open the cap just until you hear hissing to relieve the internal pressure. Then twist the cap closed and leave at room temperature until needed. When you're ready to pitch, relieve the pressure again in the same way, then close the cap, shake the vial to suspend the yeast cells, and then carefully open the cap all the way and pitch your yeast.)

3. When you are ready to pitch the yeast, sanitize the yeast packet and a pair of scissors with a brief dunk in sanitizer (no scissors needed for Wyeast Activator).

4. Open the yeast packet, using sanitized scissors if necessary, and pour the contents directly into fresh wort.

Steeping Specialty Grains and Adding Malt Extract

Specialty grains and malt extract are what make wort possible. Recall from Chapter 6 that while extract supplies most of the sugars that yeast cells will ferment into carbon dioxide and alcohol, specialty grains add color, flavor, aroma, and fresh malt character to your homebrew.

A handful of recipes have no specialty grains whatsoever, but I feel that even small amounts of specialty grains add depth that extract sometimes can't achieve on its own. If your recipe has no specialty grains, consider steeping 8 ounces (225 g) of a neutral specialty malt such as Carapils or Carafoam to get started. These add no color or fermentable sugars, but you'll gain a little fresh malt character from them.

So, get out your brew kettle, specialty grains, mesh bag, malt extract, and big spoon. Follow the instructions in "How to Steep Specialty Grains" (page 90) to get your wort off and running, and then add the malt extract according to the simple directions in "How to Add Malt Extract" (page 91).

Keep in mind that the total boil volume depends on your equipment. If you're working with a 3-gallon (11.3 l) stockpot, then 2.5 gallons (9.4 l) is about as much as you can do. On the other hand, if you have a nice big 8-gallon (30 l) crab-boil-style pot, then you can boil the entire 5-gallon (19 l) batch! Because all of your malt and extract goes into the boil kettle, boiling a smaller volume such as 2.5 gallons (9.4 l) means you'll be boiling a concentrated wort, which will later need to be topped

How to Steep Specialty Grains

1. If your specialty grains haven't been milled, use a dedicated malt mill or place them in a large zip-top plastic bag and lightly crush them using a rolling pin. All you need to do is crack the grain kernels open, so no need to go too crazy.

2. Heat a gallon (4 l) or so of water—the exact volume isn't important—in your brew kettle on the stove. While the water is heating, place the milled specialty grains into a mesh nylon or muslin bag (see page 89 for the easiest way to get grains into a mesh bag).

3. When the water reaches 160°F (70°C), kill the heat and place your mesh bag of milled grain into the hot water. Make sure to close the bag's drawstring if it has one or tie the open end of the bag onto one of the pot's handles to keep grain from floating into your hot water. Set the timer for 30 minutes and cover the brew kettle with a lid.

4. After half an hour, remove the specialty grains from the hot water (now proto-wort) and discard the grains. Spent grains are a great addition to the compost bin (and a popular staple among discerning backyard squirrels worldwide).

up with water to bring it up to the full batch size and dilute it down to the appropriate strength. Boiling the whole batch means no top-up water at the end, but it also means that you need a big heat source, which is why so many homebrewers end up buying outdoor propane burners.

Once you've added all of this malt goodness to your pot of hot water, you want to be *very* careful to avoid a boilover. Remember that the dissolved sugars and proteins have a tendency to foam up and leap right out of the kettle until you've added the first hops addition. So keep an eye on your wort and do not walk away from it!

Boiling Wort with Hops

When the wort approaches the boiling point, a silky cap will develop on top. You want to make sure to have at least a couple of inches (5 cm) of headspace between the wort and the top of the kettle so that when it starts to foam up (and it will), you have time to push it back down.

And just how do you push it back down? As I mention in Chapter 7, I've found that a two-handed approach works rather well:

- **Keep one hand on the burner knob** and reduce the heat as needed.
- **Keep a spray bottle of water in the other hand** and mist the foam on top of the wort. This cools it enough to keep it from boiling over.

How to Add Malt Extract

1. Bring your specialty grain–infused water to a boil, then shut off the heat.
2. Using a long-handled spoon or whisk, add the malt extract.
3. Stir completely to fully dissolve the malt extract in the grain water. Liquid malt extract is thick, so keep stirring until it no longer sticks to your spoon. Dry malt extract is powdery and clumpy, so consider using a whisk to help break it up and help it dissolve.
4. Congratulations, you now have wort! Turn the heat back on and bring your wort to a boil.

Eventually, that cap of foam will become unstable and fall back on itself. At this point, it's time to set the kitchen timer and let the boil begin!

The vast majority of beer you make will require a boil time of 60 minutes, but this won't always be the case. Some very light beers such as Pilsners may need 90 minutes of boil time if you brew from grain malts, but you probably won't run into this with extract. In other cases, the boil may be only half an hour. How do you know how long to boil? Here's how: The boil must last at least as long as the specified time of the first hops addition.

If your recipe specifies a first hops addition at 60 minutes (and most do), that means you'll need to boil for an hour. If that first hops addition is at 75 or 90 minutes, as may be the case for certain very bitter styles such as double IPA, then you'll need to plan on a 75- or 90-minute boil. But if your first hops addition doesn't enter the picture until the 45-minute mark, then by all means, truncate that boil down to 45 minutes. No need to boil any longer than necessary. So, let's assume here that we're boiling for an hour and the first hops addition is at 60 minutes. In that case, set your kitchen timer for 65 minutes.

Wait! What's up with the extra 5 minutes? Boiling for a few minutes before the first hops addition gives the wort a few minutes to stabilize, which I've found helps keep it from trying to boil over when you hit it with the first hops addition. It's not a complete panacea, but I think it helps.

Once you're at the 60-minute mark, add your recipe's first hops addition, called the bittering addition. Keep your hand on the burner control and be prepared to turn down the flame—or turn it completely off—to keep the wort from boiling over. Once the wort looks as if it has stabilized, leave the flame at a level that maintains a solid rolling boil.

For the next hour, your only job is to add hops at the intervals specified by your recipe. If you're brewing a classic German Hefeweizen or certain Scottish ales, the first hops addition may well have been your only one, in which case, congratulations! All you have to do is wait! An American IPA recipe may ask you to add hops every 10 minutes, even more frequently as the end of the boil draws near. Just follow the directions in your recipe.

Pay attention to the timer, but don't worry if you add hops a minute or two too late or too early. Homebrewing is more like cooking than baking when it comes to adding *Humulus lupulus*. And don't forget, hops additions are always specified in *minutes before the end of the boil*. A 5-minute addition is 5 minutes before you kill the heat, not 5 minutes after you started.

After the initial hops addition, the ebullient boil becomes better behaved, so feel free to walk away for brief periods of time to use the restroom, change the radio station, grab a beer, pet the cat, whatever. But don't stray too far. Keep one eye on the boil at all times and be prepared to jump into action should it become too enthusiastic.

I like to use this time to sanitize and prepare my equipment, but the first couple of times you brew, consider keeping a book nearby. Just make sure you add the hops when you're meant to. And don't forget to sanitize the lid to your boil kettle, as you'll need that at the end of the boil.

When about 5–10 minutes remain in the boil, prepare an ice and water bath in your kitchen sink, a large bucket, or another vessel that can hold your brew pot and a mix of ice and water. In addition to good old-fashioned ice cubes, I like to drop in a few of the frozen gel packs that ship with yeast to make sure things stay nice and cold.

If you're using a wort chiller, you can skip preparing an ice bath and instead place the chiller in your boiling wort with 10 minutes remaining in the boil.

Cooling Hot Wort to Fermentation Temperature

Once you've added your last hops addition and reached the zero mark on the timer, kill the heat. Then cover the brew kettle with a sanitized lid to keep airborne nasties from getting in there while your wort chills. Using potholders, oven mitts, or long-neglected baseball gloves, carefully lift your covered brew pot and gently lower it into the ice bath. Top up the ice bath with additional cold water if needed to keep most of the kettle submerged.

It's helpful to periodically stir the cold water and ice bath in one direction (counterclockwise, say) and then rotate the brew pot in the other (clockwise) to encourage heat transfer through the wall of the kettle. If you have enough ice to top the bath back up after the first batch melts, then do that as well. Ideally, you want to get this baby down to fermentation temperature in 20 minutes or less.

Transferring Chilled Wort to a Sanitized Fermentor

When the chilled wort drops below 68°F (20°C) or so, as measured by a sanitized thermometer, then you can stop cooling it. Actually, if you've boiled only a portion of the total batch volume, say 3 gallons of 5 (or 11 liters of 19), then you can stop when it's a few degrees warmer, as adding cold top-up water will lower the temperature even further.

Using a sanitized colander, pour your cooled wort into the sanitized fermentation bucket. Some brewers recommend using a siphon to transfer from the kettle to the bucket, but pouring through a mesh colander **(left)** helps aerate the wort, which is a critical part of ensuring healthy fermentation. Choose your favorite way to get wort from the kettle to the fermentor, but remember that some amount of splashing and agitation is a good thing at this stage. Yeast needs oxygen to start fermentation, so splash away in that bucket!

If you've boiled a concentrated wort, then you'll need to top up your fermentor to the full-batch volume, typically 5 gallons (19 l). Some will insist that you need to use water that has previously been boiled and then cooled, but I have always used cold water straight from the tap and have never had an issue. Do whatever helps you sleep best at night. Should you simply use the kitchen sink, consider taking advantage of the sprayer, if you have one, to add vital oxygen to your fermentor.

Finally—and it is critical that you not skip this step—take a specific gravity reading using your hydrometer

Of course, if you own a wort chiller, then you don't have to bother with the ice bath. Just hook up the inlet to a garden hose or your kitchen faucet, direct the outlet away from anything that can't stand a barrage of hot water, and let 'er rip. See "How to Use an Immersion Wort Chiller" (page 95) for more information about chilling your wort with a wort chiller.

How to Use an Immersion Wort Chiller

There are two main types of wort chillers: counterflow and immersion. Counterflow chillers require that you pump wort through one of the chiller's inlets at the same time as you pump cold water through the other inlet. The cold water and hot wort pass on either side of a metal plate or coil, rapidly transferring the heat of the wort to the cooling water. Because pumps (or gravity) are required, though, they can be a bit complex for the beginning homebrewer.

An immersion chiller, on the other hand, is just a coil of metal that has one inlet and one outlet. The whole coil is immersed in hot wort, and cold water is pushed into the inlet, usually via a garden hose or your kitchen sink, and it exits the chiller's outlet after having picked up heat from the wort.

Using an immersion chiller is straightforward.

1. About 10 minutes before the end of the boil, place the coil in your boiling wort. This will sanitize the chiller.
2. Attach a water source, such as a garden hose, to the inlet of the chiller.
3. Direct the chiller's outlet hose to something that heat won't harm (e.g., *not* your spouse's flower garden). Consider collecting the hot waste water in a separate vessel and using it for cleaning up after your brew, but understand that there will be a lot of waste water!
4. When you reach the end of the boil, kill the heat, and turn on the water source. Cold water will begin flowing into the chiller, and after a brief delay, hot water will emerge out the other end.
5. Using an oven mitt, grab the chiller from time to time and gently swirl it in the hot wort to enhance heat transfer.
6. When the wort reaches your desired pitching temperature, turn off the water source and remove the chiller from your wort.

How to Rack (Transfer) Your Beer

Racking beer is a task that every homebrewer has to do at least once in the life of each batch. It's nothing more than transferring beer from one vessel to another. The pros rely on pumps, and some homebrewers do, too, but most of us use gravity to move our beer, which is where siphoning comes in.

To siphon beer, you'll need the following:

- A clean, sanitized auto-siphon
- 5 feet (1.5 m) or more of clean, sanitized flexible siphon tubing
- Your beer
- A clean, sanitized carboy, bottling bucket, or a keg (depending on when you are racking your beer)

The process itself is straightforward:

1. Place the source vessel that contains your beer on a table, kitchen counter, or other elevated surface.
2. Place the destination vessel on the floor.
3. Attach one end of your flexible tubing to the internal racking cane on the auto-siphon that slides up and down inside the housing.
4. Place the other end of the tubing in the destination vessel, as near the bottom as you can.
5. Dip the sanitized auto-siphon into the beer you want to transfer, but not all the way to the bottom. Halfway is usually pretty good.
6. Gently pull up on the internal racking cane, about a foot (30 cm) or so and then push it down all the way to the bottom of the auto-siphon.

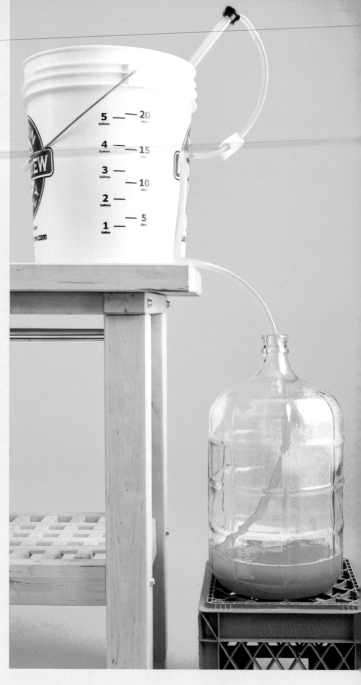

At this point, beer should flow up through the racking cane, down the siphon tubing, and into your destination vessel. If it doesn't quite make it, give the auto-siphon a couple of extra pumps. Once you've established a siphon, then gently lower the tip of the auto siphon toward the bottom of your beer. You may pick up a small amount of sediment and yeast, but that's fine.

Avoid splashing and spraying as much as you possibly can. Introducing oxygen at this stage will only stale your beer and lead to paper-like off-flavors.

When all of the beer has been transferred, you're done!

(see "How to Use a Hydrometer," page 98). Recall from Chapter 7 that this is your beer's original gravity, which tells you how much sugar is available for fermentation. It won't all get consumed, but only by knowing where you start can you possibly know where you might end up. (That sounds like something Yoda might have said.)

Pitching Yeast

With 5 gallons (19 l) of cool wort in your fermentor, it's time to pitch the yeast. See "How to Use Dry Yeast" (right) if you're using dry yeast. If you're using a Wyeast smack pack, simply tear open the top of the now-swollen pack and dump the contents right into the wort. White Labs PurePitch pouches need to be opened with sanitized scissors. If you are using the older White Labs vials that resemble test tubes, slowly twist open the cap slightly to relieve pressure, then twist it closed again. Give the vial a good shake to suspend the yeast and slowly open it all the way before pouring the contents into your wort.

Ultimately, all you need to do is get those yeast cells into your wort in a sanitary way. Then just place the sanitized lid on top of your fermentation bucket, affix the sanitized airlock, and fill the airlock with sanitizer, cheap vodka, or straight tap water. Place the fermentor in a dark, cool spot where the temperature is unlikely to exceed 68°F (20°C)—the cooler the better, down to about 60°F (16°C)—and leave it alone.

How to Use Dry Yeast

Dry yeast is convenient and reliable, and it is a cinch to use. Some manufacturers and brewers tell you to just sprinkle the contents of the yeast packet directly onto the surface of your wort, but hydrating the yeast in advance enhances viability and takes just a few minutes.

1. Add 8 ounces (250 ml) lukewarm water (about 95°F/35°C) to a sanitized measuring cup. Using sanitized scissors, cut open your sachet of dry yeast.
2. Sprinkle the contents of the sachet on top of the lukewarm water, but *do not stir*.
3. Wait 5 minutes for the yeast to absorb water, then gently agitate the measuring cup by slowly swirling it. Wait another 5 minutes, or until all of the dry grains of yeast have dissolved.
4. Swirl the slurry to suspend the yeast cells, then add the slurry to the fresh wort.

How to Use a Hydrometer

The hydrometer is your best friend when you want an answer to the question, "Is fermentation over yet or what?" While a happily bubbling airlock and a cap of foam on the fermenting beer are good signs, these are only visual cues, and it's entirely possible for fermentation to proceed without them. A hydrometer, however, does not lie.

A hydrometer measures the density of a liquid relative to that of water. So, placing a hydrometer in pure distilled water will yield a reading of 1.000. Sugar-rich wort will be considerably denser, usually in the 1.040–1.100 range, the higher, the more sugary. That number falls as the beer ferments.

It's possible to float a hydrometer in the fermentation bucket, but sometimes the scale can be hard to read. Carboys, with their narrow necks, are another story altogether: Don't even think of trying to plunk a hydrometer into one. You won't get it back out until you rack the beer, and you run the very real risk of breaking the hydrometer in the process!

The most popular alternative to measuring right in the bucket is the hydrometer test jar. These are cylinders, usually plastic, with a stable base. You just draw a sample of wort or beer, fill the jar, and then place the hydrometer inside.

The jar works great, but it's far from perfect. In order to get the beer, you either have to start a siphon (messy) or use a wine thief to remove the sample. And that brings us to my preferred tool for the job, a combination wine thief and test tube.

A traditional wine thief resembles a long turkey baster from which the squeeze bulb at the top has been removed, and it functions like a large straw. Insert the thief into your liquid of choice and place a thumb over the hole at the top to pull a sample. Then remove the thief, hold it over a sample jar. When you remove your thumb from the top of the thief, the jar fills with liquid.

A modern variant on the classic thief design has a small valve on the business end of the device that allows wort or beer to flow into the tube when it is submerged in liquid. But when you remove it, the weight of the trapped liquid closes the valve. Then you just float a hydrometer right in the thief itself, eliminating the need for a separate jar.

Here's how to use a hydrometer, whether you use a hydrometer test jar or wine thief:

- Remove a sample of wort or beer from your fermentor using a sanitized wine thief **(1 at right)**.
- If your thief doesn't let you take measurements directly inside it (see above), transfer the sample to a separate hydrometer jar.
- Gently lower the hydrometer, bulb-end down, into the sample **(2)**, and give the stem a quick swirl as you let go of it.
- Wait for the hydrometer to stop spinning, then read the specific gravity **(3)**. It's the number on the stem that corresponds to the lowest part of the meniscus. (The meniscus is the curved surface of the liquid between the walls of the tube and the surface of the hydrometer. It's caused by surface tension, which doesn't indicate specific gravity. So always read at the bottom of the meniscus for accurate results.)
- Write down the number in your notes.

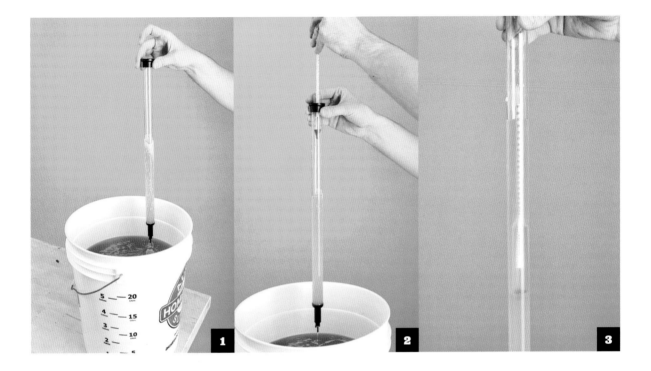

Cleaning Up

Washing up is straightforward. Use PBW or OxiClean to clean your mess. If you brewed in your kitchen and your significant other has been kind enough to tolerate your brew day without complaint, take a moment to leave the kitchen cleaner than you found it. This will go a long way toward your continued encouragement to brew beer.

FERMENTATION

Fermentation is the 1- to 2-week process during which yeast cells consume the wort sugars you've so lovingly prepared and convert them into carbon dioxide and ethanol. For the fermentation period, you need the following items:

■ **A cool, dark, quiet place** in which to ferment your beer

■ **Sanitizer** of your choice
■ **Patience**
■ **Hydrometer**
■ **Beer or wine thief**

There's very little you can do during this phase to influence the outcome once it gets going, but *you can keep your fermentor cool*, ideally 65–68°F (18–20°C).

If the seals on your bucket and airlock are in good shape, you'll probably notice bubbles issuing forth from the airlock, but it's entirely possible for beer to ferment with nary a bubble to be seen or burp to be heard. The only way to accurately measure progress is to take a hydrometer reading, a good habit into which to get.

I suggest taking as few hydrometer readings as possible because every time you open the fermentor, it's another opportunity to introduce oxygen and potential contaminants. So, give your beer at least a week before taking a measurement. Higher-gravity styles such as

reading and multiplying them by the yeast's apparent attenuation, usually available from the manufacturer's website. Then subtract that number from the original. Here's an example.

Let's say the original gravity of your beer is 1.050, and your yeast has an apparent attenuation of 70 percent. Seventy percent of 50 is 35, which means that you expect the yeast to consume 35 of the 50 gravity points. That means you'll have 50 − 35 = 15 gravity points at the end of fermentation, or a final gravity of 1.015.

Thus, if three consecutive hydrometer readings come in at or near 1.015, you can safely assume your beer is done. However, if they're closer to 1.020, you might want to wait a few more days before declaring it finished. If, after that, you're still at 1.020, then gently swirl the fermentor, warm it up to 70° (21°C), and wait again. If after *that*, fermentation still hasn't budged, you're ready for the maturation period.

MATURATION

Recall from Chapter 9 that all beer needs a maturation period, during which time its rough edges can smooth, its flavors can meld, and yeast cells can clean up after themselves. Here's what you need for this 1- to 2-week period:

- **A cool, dark, quiet place** in which to condition your beer
- **Patience**

Optional items include:

- **Sanitized carboy** with **bung** and **airlock**
- **Sanitized siphon tubing** and **auto-siphon**

Maturation could be as simple as waiting a few days after fermentation winds down, or it could be as complex as transferring to a lagering vessel and putting your beer down for a 6-month nap at a temperature near freezing. For your first batch, I suggest simply leaving

Belgian tripels and imperial anythings are probably best given 2 weeks.

If your beer's specific gravity, as measured with a hydrometer, remains constant over separate readings taken 3 days in a row, then your beer has probably finished fermenting. I say *probably* because there is a possibility, especially with certain yeast strains, that you'll experience stuck fermentation, which is when the yeast gives up prematurely and fails to fully ferment the wort.

How do you know if fermentation is truly complete or simply stuck? Calculate your expected final gravity (FG) and see if the current gravity reading is close. You can estimate the expected FG by taking the numbers to the right of the 1 in the original gravity (OG)

your beer alone for a couple of extra weeks. You'll avoid possible oxidation and contamination and increase the likelihood that your first batch will be a success.

That said, I know that you're probably also eager to get started on your next batch of homebrew, which means you need that fermentation vessel! In that case, it's worth racking to a secondary vessel, typically a 5-gallon (19 l) carboy. See "How to Rack (Transfer) Your Beer" (page 96) for details on how to do this. If you do transfer your beer into a clear vessel such as a carboy, be sure to store it in a dark place or wrap it in an old towel or sheet **(left)** to keep out light, which could turn your beer skunky.

Once your beer is in its maturation vessel, leave it alone until you're ready to bottle.

BOTTLING

Bottling day is at once exciting and frustrating. It's exciting because you're well on your way to enjoying your homebrew, but frustrating because you still have to wait another 2–3 weeks to taste it. But it's the last thing standing between you and your beer, so get to it! Here's what you need:

- **Sanitizer** of your choice
- 6.5-gallon (25 l) **bottling bucket** with integrated spigot
- Enough clean, sanitized **bottles** to hold all of your homebrew (see Chapter 4 for how to sanitize bottles in the oven or dishwasher; see Chapter 10 for the quantity of longnecks, bombers, and European half liters you'll need)
- An equivalent number of **bottle caps,** often called crown caps
- **Auto-siphon**
- Plastic **siphon tubing,** about 5 feet (1.5 m), preferably with a pinch clamp
- **Bottling wand**
- **Small saucepan**
- 4–5 ounces (113–142 g) of **corn sugar** (dextrose); your local homebrew store may sell priming sugar in bulk

or in 5-ounce (142 g) bags. As you gain experience, you may want to adjust the amount of sugar you use to achieve different carbonation levels for different styles of beer. But when you're just getting started, 4 or 5 ounces (113–142 g) is a good general-purpose amount.
- **Bottle capper**
- **Something to drink** while you fill bottles

Use the small saucepan to boil 5 ounces (140 g) of corn sugar in 2 cups (16 fl oz/475 ml) of water for 5 minutes. Remove from the heat, place a lid on top, and leave to cool while you prepare for bottling. While the sugar water is cooling, sanitize all of your equipment except the bottle capper.

Now it's time to transfer your beer to the bottling bucket, a food-grade plastic bucket with a spigot near the bottom. Use your auto-siphon and tubing to gently rack the beer into the bottling bucket (see "How to Rack (Transfer) Your Beer," page 96). Keep this process nice and smooth, and avoid splashing as much as possible. Some splashing is bound to happen, but racking quietly means less oxygen to spoil your beer.

As the beer flows into the bottling bucket, gently pour the sugar solution on top of it. When all the beer has been transferred, remove the siphon equipment and raise the bottling bucket up to a tabletop or countertop that's above the area where you plan to fill bottles.

Let the primed beer sit for 5 minutes or so to give any particulates time to settle to the bottom. This also helps the priming solution evenly mix throughout the beer, ensuring even carbonation from one bottle to the next.

When it's time to fill bottles, attach one end of a sanitized length of siphon tubing to a sanitized bottling wand and the other end to the sanitized spigot on your bottling bucket. Place several sanitized bottles in a row on the floor or—even better—on the lower rack of your open dishwasher. You can line up as many as you're comfortable with, but many brewers fill six or twelve bottles at a time because that many bottles fit neatly into 6-pack and 12-pack holders, respectively.

Open the spigot on the bottling bucket and place the bottling wand into your first bottle. Press the tip lightly onto the bottom of the bottle to start the flow of beer. Keep an eye on it as the bottle fills so that it doesn't overflow! When the beer just reaches the lip of the bottle, pull up on the wand and remove it from the bottle. The volume that the wand displaces leaves just the right amount of headspace when you remove the wand from the bottle.

Continue this process until you have bottled the entire batch. You should get somewhere between forty-eight and fifty-two 12-ounce (355 ml) bottles out of a 5-gallon (19 l) batch. If you don't have enough beer to fill the last bottle more than about two-thirds full, then drink the flat beer and save the bottle for your next batch. Leaving too much head space in the bottle could lead to over-carbonation and an explosion!

Capping your bottles is a piece of cake. Just place a sanitized crown cap on the bottle capper's magnetized bell, lower the bell onto the top of the bottle. Pushing down on the capper's two wings engages a pair of metal plates that grasp the bottle's neck on either side while simultaneously plunging the bell down and onto the cap. When the two wings snap down to become horizontal and parallel to the bottling surface, the cap seats firmly onto the bottle, and you're done. Be careful, though. The bottles may be wet and could easily slide out from under you and break as you push down with the capper. Consider bottling on a kitchen towel to mop up liquids and offer some grip to the bottle.

After you have capped all of your bottles, dry them off, and store them away in a spot that is at or slightly above room temperature. Consider placing them in a large bin or tub with a lid just in case one of the bottles explodes.

Put those bottles away for *at least 2 weeks.* I know how tempting it is to crack open that first bottle, but it's important to give the yeast enough time to carbonate your homebrew. Your patience will be rewarded with better beer. Two weeks minimum. Three is even better!

Pro tip: Why not brew up another batch of homebrew while you're waiting?

SERVING

Everything you have done until now has been in service of this moment when you can sample your beer. Here is what you need:

- One or more bottles of **homebrew**
- A **refrigerator**
- A **bottle opener**
- A carefully selected **glass** appropriate for the occasion (see Chapter 11)
- A couple of **friends,** if you're feeling generous

At least 24 hours before you plan to open your first few bottles, put them in the refrigerator.

Why wait 24 hours? It doesn't take that long to chill a bottle of beer, after all. No, but it *does* take time for carbon dioxide in the headspace to dissolve into the beer beneath it. You could accelerate the process by shaking the bottle once it's at the right temperature, but this is likely to upset your friends when they pop the top.

So, 3 weeks of conditioning, and then 24 hours in the fridge. Now it's time.

Pull your beer from the refrigerator and pop off the cap using your preferred method: bottle opener, wedding ring, flat-head screwdriver, incantations, whatever. Listen for the hiss. If it's there, it means you have carbonation! If not, pull the remaining bottles from the fridge and bring them up to room temperature to condition for another couple of weeks.

If you have carbonation, pour your beer into a glass, taking care to leave the small bit of sediment behind (unless you brewed a Hefeweizen, in which case swirl up all that yeast and dump it into the glass. It's part of the experience!).

Observe the color, bubbles, and aroma as you pour. No need to write anything down unless you really want to. Just notice what you see.

And then drink your beer.

That's it.

That's all there is.

Part III

All-Grain Brewing

Chapter 13

An Introduction to All-Grain Brewing

Taste every fruit of every tree in the garden at least once. It is an insult to creation not to experience it fully. Temperance is wickedness.
– Stephen Fry

Every child is an artist. The problem is staying an artist when you grow up.
– Pablo Picasso

IN ALL-GRAIN BREWING, YOU PREPARE wort by mashing malted grain. You forego the convenience of malt extract in exchange for having more influence over your beer. Some might have you believe that all-grain brewing is superior to extract brewing. It's not. It's simply another way to prepare wort and fulfill the third of the eight essential steps.

The difference between all-grain brewing and extract brewing is similar to the difference between making your own soup from scratch and reconstituting condensed soup from a can. You end up with soup either way, but making your own gives you more control and tastes fresher. Here are a few reasons to go all-grain.

- You have complete say over wort composition and aren't limited to the malt extract that manufacturers sell. Most Munich extracts are, for example, made from 50 percent Munich malt and 50 percent pale malt. With all-grain brewing, you can make wort from 100 percent Munich malt if you want.
- You gain access to certain malts that aren't available

as extracts. While extracts of English Maris Otter malt and Vienna malt are now available, the Scottish malt Golden Promise has no extract counterpart nor do some varieties of Munich malt. All-grain brewers can also choose to include adjuncts such as maize, oats, and rice.

- You gain a deeper understanding of beer. When you mash your own grain, you begin to notice subtle changes in wort composition that may not have previously been apparent. You'll understand enzymes and how minor tweaks to the mash can translate into major differences in the finished product.
- You can brew beer that is very light in color. Extract-based beer is almost always a little darker than beer made fresh from grain. Extract begins life a little dark to begin with and continues to deepen in color as it ages.

All-grain brewing is fun and rewarding, but it's not for everyone. Here are a few things to consider before you jump in.

- All-grain brewing requires more equipment—not *a lot* more equipment, but more nonetheless. This may be an issue for those who live in small spaces.
- All-grain brewing requires more time. There's no getting around this. An experienced brewer who prepares a few things in advance might be able to finish in 4–5 hours, but expect your first all-grain brew day to take 6–8 hours.
- All-grain brewing requires more heat. If you're already brewing on a propane burner, this won't be an issue, but if you're accustomed to boiling 3–4 gallons of concentrated wort on your kitchen stove and topping up with water, you'll need to procure a heat source that can bring 6–7 gallons of wort to a rolling boil.
- All-grain brewing requires more attention. There are simply more variables to consider when mashing your own grain. When you understand them, you can manipulate them to your advantage, but they also provide more opportunities for unintended consequences.

Even if you plan to stick with extract for the foreseeable future, I encourage you to read this section. You'll gain a greater understanding of how brewing works, and you'll be better prepared down the road should you decide to give all-grain methods a try.

EQUIPMENT REQUIREMENTS

The basic equipment required for all-grain brewing includes everything you need for extract brewing, plus a few additional pieces. You can purchase ready-made all-grain equipment from homebrew retailers, or you can build your own. The pieces you need are

- **Mash-lauter tun**
- **Hot-liquor tank**
- **Heat source**
- **Wort chiller** (if you don't already have one)

Mash-Lauter Tun

The *mash-lauter tun* is where all of the action happens. It is here that you combine crushed grain with hot water in a process called *mashing*. After the starches have been converted to sugars, it is also the scene of *lautering*, or separating the sweet wort from the spent grain.

In large breweries, the mash tun and lauter tun are separate vessels. Pumping the mash from a dedicated mash tun to a dedicated lauter tun frees up the mash tun for the next batch. At home, however, it's unlikely that you would ever brew back-to-back in this fashion. Thus, for homebrewers (and many small craft brewers), mashing and lautering take place in the same tun, the cleverly named mash-lauter tun, or MLT.

A mash-lauter tun has just a few requirements:

- It must be physically capable of holding the mash.
- It must be able to maintain a specified temperature for at least an hour.
- It must provide some means of straining sweet wort from the grain.

The most affordable MLT option for most hobbyists is to use a plastic beverage cooler **(right)**. For 5-gallon (19 l) batches, a cooler of the same size will allow you to comfortably brew beers up to about 1.060 original gravity. Higher gravity means more grain, which means more volume. Thus, 10-gallon (38 l) models are popular as well. An insulated cooler will hold a mixture of crushed grain and hot water within the desired temperature range for at least a couple of hours with only a degree or two of loss.

To separate out the wort, a filtering device is placed in the bottom of the cooler and connected to a ball valve through which wort can flow. There are numerous types of filters, but the false bottom is among the most versatile **(page 107).** This is little more than a slightly domed screen that keeps the grain bed just off the bottom of the tun. Wort is removed from below the false bottom and sent out through the valve.

Hot-Liquor Tank

The term *hot-liquor tank (HLT)* sounds dramatic (who among us couldn't go for some hot liquor on a cold winter's night?), but it's nothing more than a tank that holds hot water. Fancy, eh?

Now to be fair, brewers make a distinction between water and liquor. Water is untreated H_2O that comes from the source, while brewing liquor is water that has been treated in some way to make it suitable for brewing. If the water in your area is suitable for mashing, your hot liquor is simply tap water that has been heated.

The HLT is commonly, though not necessarily, the same volume as the mash tun. Many brewers use a second beverage cooler without a false bottom. My

HLT is about as simple as it gets: an 8-gallon (30 l) aluminum stockpot **(below)** in which I heat water.

Heat Source

If you've been brewing on your kitchen stove, then moving to all-grain brewing may mean investing in a bigger heat source. In all-grain brewing, we collect the *entire* batch of wort, which for most of us means 5 gallons (19 l) or so. Actually, if you account for evaporation over the course of an hour or more (which you should), then it really means collecting closer to 6.5 gallons (25 l).

Most residential kitchen stoves don't supply enough heat to bring that much water to a rolling boil in a reasonable amount of time. Some brewers manage by straddling a brew kettle across two burners, but most brewers take the operation outside and use a propane burner or turkey fryer.

Wort Chiller

Some extract brewers never purchase a wort chiller. I never bothered with one until I started brewing all-grain. Even now, when I brew from extract (about a quarter of the time), I boil a concentrated wort on the stovetop and dunk it into an ice bath to cool.

But when you need to drop 5 gallons (19 l) or more of boiling hot wort by 150°F (83°C) in a short amount of time, a dedicated wort chiller is the way to go.

The most commonly used wort chiller is the immersion chiller. It's a large coil of copper or stainless-steel tubing that is placed in boiling wort for a few minutes to heat sanitize. Then, when the boil is complete, cold water is run through the coil, which pulls heat from the wort and carries

it out of the chiller as hot wastewater (which can be collected and used for cleaning). A wort chiller can usually bring 5 gallons (19 l) of wort down to pitching temperature in about 15 minutes.

THE ALL-GRAIN PROCESS

All-grain brewing really ought to be called all-grain wort preparation because extract and all-grain brewing share all of the eight steps and differ only in the execution of the third step. Thus, everything you know from extract brewing remains valid for all-grain methods. You just need a different Step 3. Here's how it goes.

1. Grain malts are crushed to expose the inner starches for conversion.
2. Crushed grain is mixed with hot water in the mash-lauter tun and allowed to rest at a single temperature or, in some cases, at a sequence of increasingly warmer temperatures. This process is the mash, and it results in the conversion of starch to sugar.
3. After conversion, the wort is drained from the grain in a process called lautering. But a good deal of sugar remains stuck to the grain, so the grain is rinsed with additional hot water in a process called sparging.
4. The runoff from lautering and sparging is collected in the boil kettle until the desired volume is achieved. Then the boil proceeds as usual.

That's all there is to it. We'll cover a few more of the details in Chapters 14 and 15, but that's all-grain wort preparation in a nutshell.

PARTIAL-MASH METHODS

Finally, all-grain doesn't have to be all or nothing. Partial-mash is an attractive alternative for brewers who want to experiment with grain without fully committing to the full complexity of all-grain methods. Some of the advantages to partial-mash brewing include:

- Minimal equipment needs. You can conduct a small mash in your brew kettle and simply top it up with extract and water before the boil.
- Minimal time commitment. Extracting a small volume of wort from a tiny mash takes a fraction of the time that is needed to collect the full 6.5 gallons (25 l) normally required for a 5-gallon (19 l) batch of all-grain beer.
- Freshness. Mashing even a small amount of grain introduces fresh flavors and aromas that you sometimes can't achieve with extract and specialty grains alone.
- Access to special malts. A partial-mash brewer can incorporate rye, Munich, Vienna, Golden Promise, and other malts that may be difficult or impossible to obtain as extracts.
- Access to unmalted adjuncts. Grains that aren't malted lack the enzymes to convert starches to sugars. Flaked oats, for example, won't contribute much to a stout if they're just steeped in hot water. But when mashed with enzyme-rich pale malt, oats transform a regular stout into a silky oatmeal stout.

If you'd like to try your hand at partial-mash methods, just use the same principles we discuss in the upcoming chapters to mash a small quantity of grain and continue as you normally would with extract brewing.

MOVING ON

All-grain wort preparation methods are nothing more than a different means to the same end. If you enjoy brewing and want to get closer to your ingredients and have more control, it may be for you. But if you want to keep things simple, extract always remains a viable approach. Still, understanding some all-grain basics will give you greater insight into the brewing process from grain to glass.

Chapter 14

Mashing Basics

"This–this is merely my way–Where is yours?" I thus answered those who asked about The Way. "For The Way does not exist!"
– Friedrich Nietzsche, Also sprach Zarathustra

MASHING GRAIN IS WHAT MAKES beer beer. Yes, hops, yeast, and water certainly play important roles, but it is only through the mash, whether performed in your house or in the process of manufacturing malt extract, that the soul of beer is liberated from its starchy origins.

Mashing grain is to beer as crushing grapes is to wine, as pressing apples is to cider, and as collecting honey is to mead. It is the fundamental process that makes beer possible, the method by which brewers use naturally occurring enzymes in malted barley to convert starches into fermentable sugars.

In this chapter, we cover the basics of mashing your own grain. Much more can be (and has been) written on this topic than we could possibly begin to cover here, but the lessons you learn here will get you off on the right foot and serve you well for many batches to come.

WHAT THE MASH DOES

What happens when hot water and crushed grain come together is incredibly complex, and this book is far too brief to even attempt an in-depth treatise on mashing grain. But just as one need not understand the workings of the internal combustion engine to drive a car, one needn't necessarily understand every aspect of mashing grain to make great beer.

Several processes are at work during the mashing of malt, but the number one process you need be concerned with is the *conversion of starches to sugars.* And this conversion comes down to two fundamental enzymes:

- Alpha amylase (α-amylase)
- Beta amylase (β-amylase)

Alpha amylase does its best work in the 150–160°F (66–71°C) temperature range. It converts complex starches into long chains of sugars. Yeast doesn't readily ferment such sugars, so a mash temperature that favors alpha amylase tends to create less fermentable wort, which leaves residual body and sweetness in the final beer.

Beta amylase is most active in the 130–150°F (54–66°C) temperature range. It works by snipping the ends off long-chain sugars to create simpler sugars. Yeasts can easily ferment these simple sugars, so a mash that favors beta amylase will yield more fermentable wort, giving the final beer a drier finish and thinner body.

Thus, adjusting the mash temperature warmer or cooler affects the body and sweetness of the final beer by favoring alpha or beta amylase, respectively. If you really get into all-grain brewing, you'll encounter plenty of other enzymes, but these are the only two you need to know about to get started.

CRUSHING GRAIN

Malt needs to be milled, or crushed, before it can be mashed to extract fermentable sugars. In general, finely crushed malt yields better efficiency than coarsely crushed malt, but this isn't the whole story. The outer husks of barley kernels are an important part of the lautering (wort separation) process, so you want to keep those as intact as possible.

A crush that is too fine turns the internal starch into flour and shreds the barley husks into small pieces. A fine crush boosts extract efficiency, but the damaged husks are less able to filter the wort, making lautering difficult. Too coarse a crush causes the opposite problem. Intact barley husks make for easy lautering, but the starchy endosperm remains intact as well, which means that alpha and beta amylase can't easily get to the starch.

A good crush, therefore, strikes a compromise, combining acceptable extract efficiency with good lautering properties. It minimizes the sizes of the crushed starch kernels and maximizes the sizes of the husks. The malt mill at your homebrew store is probably set to strike this compromise. If you have a malt mill at home, you can experiment with various settings to achieve the perfect compromise for your system.

Commercial breweries often wet mill their malt, which involves hydrating dry malt with hot water or steam as it enters the mill. This makes the malt husks more pliable, which helps them remain intact as the starchy endosperm is crushed into fine pieces. You can achieve similar results by spritzing your malt with a spray bottle 20 minutes or so before crushing it. Just give the malt a good mist, stir, and repeat until it feels slightly moist. Not wet, just damp—"less dry," even. Then crush your malt as usual.

MASHING

Brewers create different kinds of wort by following what is called a mash schedule, mash regimen, or mash protocol. With knowledge of how different enzymes work, an advanced brewer can favor each enzyme for varying lengths of time. A mash schedule is just a timetable of different temperature steps, called rests, and how long each rest should be held.

Single-Temperature Infusion Mashing

Most all-grain homebrewers (and, for that matter, most American and British craft brewers) depend almost exclusively upon the single-temperature infusion mash. It's all you need to brew most styles of beer with well-modified malts (see Chapter 2 for more about malt modification).

In a single-infusion mash, you add (infuse) a specified quantity of hot water to crushed malt to achieve a specific mash temperature. The mash is held at that temperature for an hour or so, then the mash is complete. Changing the temperature of the mash changes the fermentability of the wort. As I discuss above, a temperature of 146–152°F (63–67°C) favors beta amylase, yielding wort that is relatively dry and light-bodied. A low mash temperature is perfect for many Belgian ales and refreshing summer lagers.

A mash in the range of 152–158°F (67–70°C) favors alpha amylase, which results in beer with lots of body and residual sweetness. A high mash temperature is ideal for any beer where a thick, viscous body is desired, including many British styles and so-called "session" beers.

Most of the beer you make will use a rest around 152–154°F (67–68°C), which offers a good compromise of beta amylase and alpha amylase activity. This is a great temperature to aim for if you don't want to think about it too much.

Multistep Temperature Mash

In a multistep temperature mash, the mash is carried through a series of rests, or temperatures, that are held for a certain period of time. A typical mash regimen might include the following:

- A **protein rest** at 113–130°F (45–54°C)
- A **beta amylase** rest at 140–150°F (60–65°C)
- An **alpha amylase rest** at 160–165°F (71–74°C)
- **Mash-out** at 170°F (77°C)

Such a mash protocol is most appropriate when the malt isn't fully modified or for brewers interested in German brewing practices. Homebrewers who want to execute a stepped temperature mash typically use a direct-fired mash tun or similar vessel to raise the mash temperature through the various steps. With some planning, homebrewers who mash in an insulated cooler can pull off a multistep mash by adding infusions of boiling water to achieve the steps.

Mashing Logistics

Strike water is the name given to the brewing liquor that is mixed with the crushed grain to start the mash. Typically, strike water is heated to several degrees above the target mash temperature. The precise temperature of the strike water depends on the temperature of your grain, the temperature of your mash tun, and even the mash tun shape, size, and material.

It's worth the small outlay of cash to purchase good-

quality brewing software to help you make these calculations. But when you're just getting started, estimating a strike temperature that's about 10–15°F (6–8°C) hotter than your intended mash temperature should get you close. When your strike water has reached the right temperature, it's time to mash in. Rather than add all of the grain and water to your mash tun at once, I recommend combining them in stages:

1. Add half the strike water to the mash tun.
2. Add half the crushed grain and stir well to mix.
3. Add the remaining strike water to the mash tun.
4. Add the remaining grain and stir well to mix.

After you've mashed in, let the mash rest for 5 minutes, then check the temperature. If it's too low, add some boiling water to raise it. If it's too high, toss in a handful of ice cubes to lower it. The mash tun should maintain the temperature throughout the mash, so

once it has stabilized, there's no need to keep checking.

Don't worry if your mash comes in a couple of degrees low or high. With experience you'll learn how to predict this. For now, as long as your mash is somewhere between 150°F (66°C) and 155°F (68°C), that's good enough.

About 20 minutes before the mash is finished, start heating sparge water (more about the sparge in the next chapter). The amount of sparge water you need changes from one batch to another, so always heat a little more than you think you'll need. The target temperature for sparge water is 168–170°F (75–77°C).

When Is the Mash Complete?

Many homebrewers make great beer without ever checking that the mash has fully converted. If you buy crushed malt from your local homebrew store and ensure that the mash temperature remains within a few degrees of the target temperature, then an hour-long mash should result in sufficient conversion in most cases.

Nonetheless, if you'd like to check for conversion, doing so is simple. You need some tincture of iodine (available at drugstores) or some undiluted Iodophor sanitizer:

1. Remove a small sample of wort from the mash tun and place it on a white saucer, taking care to remove only liquid and no grain material.
2. Add a single drop of iodine or Iodophor to the wort sample and mix thoroughly.
3. If the iodine turns black, a good deal of residual starch remains in the mash, and you should leave it for another 15–30 minutes. If the iodine remains yellow-red, then the starches have been fully converted.

The color can be difficult to discern for dark wort (such as stout), and the iodine test is far from perfect. But if you're nervous about conversion, it may help reassure you.

A FEW NOTES ON WATER

Water chemistry is a topic unto itself and can easily fill an entire volume. (In fact, it does. See *Water: A Comprehensive Guide for Brewers* by John Palmer and Colin Kaminski.)

But water quality is crucial to all-grain brewing, so you can't ignore it altogether. A few styles such as Czech Pilsener, Irish stout, and Burton IPA may benefit from a sophisticated understanding of water chemistry. But it's better to start simply and adjust your process as you gain experience than to worry about water from the outset.

Resist the temptation to start adding this and that to your water because you read somewhere that Burton water has so many parts per million (ppm) of sulfate, and yours only has 4 ppm. Tweaking ions certainly affects the flavor of your beer, but this should be a secondary consideration to *mash pH*.

Mash pH

The pH is roughly a measure of how acidic a substance is. To understand pH as a beginning brewer, you need to know only four things:

- A solution with a pH of less than 7 is said to be **acidic.**
- A solution with a pH of exactly 7 is said to be **neutral.** Pure water has a pH of 7.
- A solution with a pH higher than 7 is said to be **basic.**
- The optimal pH for a mash of malt and water is in the range of **5.2–5.6.**

Chemists can dig into textbooks to understand why this is the case. The rest of us need only remember that when we measure the pH of a mash, we want it to be in the 5.2–5.6 range. Given this ideal range and given that dissolved substances can affect that pH, our main goal as brewers is to ensure that the blend of dissolved ions and molecules results in a mash pH that's in our target range. And the two biggest players are calcium and bicarbonate:

- **Calcium** (Ca^{+2}) generally lowers mash pH. It helps alpha amylase work better at starch conversion. It even aids in settling trub and yeast at the end of fermentation. You want calcium on your side.
- **Bicarbonate** (HCO_3^{-1}) generally raises mash pH. It reduces fermentability. And it discourages sedimentation. In other words, bicarbonate is not usually your friend.

At the risk of oversimplifying a very complex situation, calcium and bicarbonate play opposite roles. By tweaking these two ions, you can often move a mash pH into the desirable range of 5.2–5.6. Here, then, is the approach I recommend you take to brewing water as a beginning homebrewer.

- **Obtain** a city water report or purchase clean, uncomplicated water if your tap water is unsuitable.

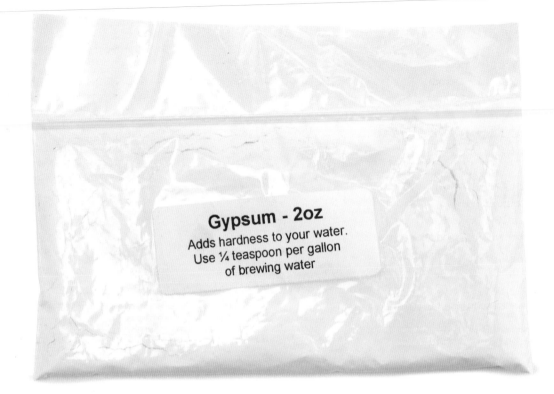

Gypsum - 2oz
Adds hardness to your water.
Use ¼ teaspoon per gallon
of brewing water

You don't know where you need to go if you don't know where you start!

- **Determine** whether your water, combined with the grain you intend to mash, falls into the pH range of 5.2–5.6.
- **Treat** your water to move the mash pH where you want it.

If your tap water is very low in mineral content, congratulations! You can brew just about anything you like by adding things to it. If, on the other hand, your tap water has a very high concentration of dissolved substances, just start with distilled or reverse osmosis (RO) water that you purchase from the store.

Remember that it's the *mash pH* that matters, not the pH of the water you add. Most water has a pH greater than 7, while grain malts contribute acidity. Generally speaking, the darker the grain, the more acidity it will lend to the mash. Very light malts, however, may not

be acidic enough to get the pH of the mash down into that 5.2–5.6 range.

The most accurate and easiest way to measure mash pH is to invest in a digital pH meter. However, pH meters don't come cheap, and they can be somewhat fussy in terms of maintenance, requiring periodic calibration. A decent alternative is to use pH test strips designed for brewing. Simply dunk the end of the strip into your mash and compare the resulting color against a scale on the side of the package. It'll get you in the ballpark.

How to adjust pH

The following additions can be used to acidify the mash (lower pH):

- **Gypsum** ($CaSO_3$) is best used in styles that benefit from hard water. Think Irish and English ales, including Irish stout and Burton IPAs.

- **Calcium chloride** ($CaCl_2$) is more neutral and is the preferred way to introduce calcium without also adding sulfate.

If you happen to need to raise the mash pH, then turn to these:

- **Baking soda** ($NaHCO_3$) raises mash pH and contributes sodium.
- **Chalk** ($CaCO_3$) can also raise the pH, but it's not as effective as baking soda. However, it's good to consider in cases where baking soda might lend too much sodium.
- **Calcium hydroxide** ($Ca(OH)_2$) must be handled carefully, but it is very effective at raising mash pH. Look for pickling lime in the canning section of your supermarket or *cal* in Latin markets—it's the substance involved in the nixtamalization of maize to make masa harina.

If your overall water profile looks good, but you're having trouble hitting the desired mash pH, you can also adjust mash acidity using other kinds of products.

- **Sauermalz,** or acidulated malt **(below left),** is a German pilsner malt that has been acidified using naturally occurring *Lactobacillus* bacteria. The German *Reinheitsgebot* prohibits water additions, but Sauermalz can drop the pH without such additions. Simply substitute a portion of the base malt with Sauermalz. Roughly speaking, a grist containing 1 percent Sauermalz will experience a 0.1 drop in pH. Two percent drops the pH by 0.2, and so on.
- **Lactic acid** is available in an 88 percent pure form from most homebrew stores. Only a few drops are needed, and it's very effective. Add a drop or two, stir the mash, and test the pH.

Chlorine

Chlorine has done wonders for modern sanitation and is incredibly effective at eliminating waterborne pathogens such as cholera. Unfortunately, chlorine can interact with compounds found in malt and create dull, plastic-like flavors in your beer. If you start with bottled water, then you don't need to worry about chlorine, but those who draw from municipal sources may need to take steps to eliminate it.

The easiest way to remove chlorine from your brewing water is to simply draw your water from the tap the day before you plan to use it and let it stand overnight. Chlorine will naturally escape into the air. Boiling accelerates this evaporation.

Unfortunately, many municipalities have switched to using a combination of chlorine and ammonia, which react to create what are known as chloramines. An effective way to reduce chloramine levels in your water is to add potassium metabisulfite, also known as Campden tablets. Usually half a tablet will do the trick for a 5-gallon (19 l) batch.

To use a Campden tablet to remove chloramines from your tap water, draw the entire volume of water that needs to be treated, including mash, sparge, and top-up water. For a 5-gallon (19 l) batch, this is usually around 8–10 gallons (30–38 l), depending upon the grain bill (more grain means more water lost to absorption). Crush half a Campden tablet into powder and add it to the water. The reaction takes only a couple of minutes, but just to be safe, wait for 5 to 10 minutes before you begin heating the water for mashing and sparging.

MOVING ON

Once your mash has completed conversion, it's time to move on to the next step: lautering. This is the process by which we separate the barley sugar water from the spent grain and collect it for brewing.

Chapter 15

Collecting Wort

Man, being reasonable, must get drunk; the best of life is but intoxication.
– Lord Byron, Don Juan, Canto II

AFTER MASHING IS COMPLETE, WE must extract wort sugars from the grain bed. This involves two processes: lautering and sparging. These two terms are collectively referred to simply as *runoff*.

Lautering is the physical separation of liquid from the solids. *Sparging* involves rinsing the solids that remain with hot water so as to leave behind as little sugar as possible. The combination of lautering the grain and sparging it with additional water results in a kettle full of wort that is ready to be boiled with hops, just as you would if you were using extract.

LAUTERING

Lautering comes from the German *läutern*, meaning to clarify, clear, or refine. Lautering takes place after the mash and refers to the process by which wort is separated from the grain bed and collected in the brew kettle. It begins with Vorlauf and ends when the final mash runnings dribble into the kettle.

Vorlauf is the first step in lautering. Another German word, it refers to the initial runnings from the mash-lauter tun, which contain particulates from the mash. Although such particles won't necessarily damage the final beer, it's best to minimize the husk material that ends up in the boil kettle. Too much husk could translate to astringency in the finished beer.

Vorlauf runnings are best collected in a measuring cup or pitcher. A capacity of 2 quarts (2 l) should be plenty. Carefully opening the valve to the mash-lauter

tun, you collect these initial runnings and observe the clarity of the flow. Once the wort is running relatively clear—which is to say, no chunks of grain—the flow is diverted to the boil kettle to collect the first runnings.

The small amount of wort collected during Vorlauf is then carefully poured back on top of the grain bed **(right)** so that it has an opportunity to filter through the husks and emerge as clear wort. You do this as gently as possible so as not to disturb the grain.

You may have to repeat this several times for the wort to run clear. Although we use the term "clear," it's likely that the wort will be rather cloudy, but it should be free of grain chunks.

With the wort running clearly and the outflow of the lauter tun flowing into the boil kettle, it's possible to slowly open the valve a little farther to speed up the process. Do this very slowly and don't tempt fate. If the liquid gets moving too quickly, the grain bed may compact, leading to a stuck mash that is reluctant to give up its precious liquid. With practice, you'll learn how far you can open the valve on your system: Some are more permissive than others.

After the initial runnings have drained from the mash tun, it's time to sparge. Close the valve and move on!

SPARGING

The word *sparge* comes from the Latin *spargere*, meaning "to sprinkle or scatter." In most commercial breweries, hot water is sprinkled over the grain bed during lautering to rinse the mashed grains of residual malt sugars. Among homebrewers, *sparging* is used more generically to describe any method of rinsing malt sugars from the mash, whether or not any sprinkling actually occurs. Three methods are popular:

- **Batch sparging** is a technique practiced, to the best of my knowledge, exclusively by homebrewers. Rather than continuously sprinkling hot water over the grain bed during lautering, one or two batches of hot water are added to the grain and then drained into the kettle. Batch sparging has the potential to be slightly less efficient than fly sparging, but it is fast. And with practice, it can yield results that are just as good as traditional methods.
- **Fly sparging,** also called continuous or German sparging, is the traditional method by which hot water is sprinkled over the grain bed as it is lautered. This process generally extracts more available sugars than other methods, but it is slow and can take an hour or more at homebrew scales.
- **No sparging** is relatively uncommon, and we won't cover it in any depth. But it's worth being familiar with it. In no-sparge methods, grain is mashed using *the entire batch's volume of water* instead of dividing the water between mash and sparge. While this process saves time, it does so at the cost of efficiency, meaning more grain is needed to produce wort of the same strength as batch and fly methods.

Batch Sparge

Many homebrewers batch sparge instead of fly sparge. Batch sparging is a variation on the traditional British practice of *parti-gyle* brewing, through which (I'm oversimplifying here for brevity's sake) different beers were produced from each set of runnings. The first runnings might become a barleywine, the second runnings a pale ale, and the third runnings an ordinary bitter. Batch sparging simply combines all of the runnings together into a single wort.

To execute a batch sparge, measure the volume of wort you collected in the first runnings and subtract it from the total batch volume. Let's say you are brewing 5 gallons (19 l) of beer with an expected pre-boil volume of 6.5 gallons (24.6 l), which means you need 6.5 gallons (24.6 l) total. Here's the process to follow after the mash.

1. When the mash is complete, open the valve to the mash-lauter tun and collect first runnings until the wort runs clear. Cloudy wort is fine. Chunks of grain are not.
2. When the wort starts to run clear, direct the flow into your boil kettle.
3. Gently pour those initial chunky runnings back on top of the grain bed.
4. When the first runnings have been collected, close the valve and measure the volume you've collected. Let's say you collected 1 gallon (3.8 l) of wort in the first runnings. You need 5.5 gallons (20.8 l) more of hot (170°F/77°C) sparge water.
5. Add half of the total sparge water (2.75 gal/10.4 l) to the mash. Stir thoroughly and wait 5 minutes for the grain to settle.
6. Repeat steps 1 and 2, first collecting a small amount of wort until it runs clear, then run the wort off into the boil kettle to mix with the first runnings. These are your second runnings. As before, gently add the chunky wort back to the top of the grain bed.
7. Repeat once more with the remaining sparge water (2.75 gal/10.4 l) to collect a set of third runnings.
8. You should now have 6.5 gallons (24.6 l) of wort that you can boil with hops!

I recommend that brewers start with batch sparging because it's easy and requires little additional equipment. Continuous (fly) sparging is a little trickier because hot water is sprinkled over the top of the grain bed *at the same time* as wort is drained from the bottom. The flow rates of the incoming water and outgoing wort have to match to keep the grain bed from becoming compacted.

1

When done correctly, fly sparging sets up a continuous flow of ever-weaker wort. Sparging continues until the desired volume of wort is collected, or until the specific gravity of the outflow drops below 1.008–1.010. Over-sparging, which means continuing to sparge after the gravity of the runoff falls below this threshold, can extract undesirable compounds from the husks that lend an astringent flavor to your homebrew.

MOVING ON

That's it! Lautering and sparging aren't mysterious, despite the esoteric names. They're simply methods to get as much wort as possible out of your mash.

And with an end to lautering and sparging comes the end of the all-grain process. All-grain is just another way to satisfy the third of the essential steps, wort preparation. Once you have a kettle full of fresh wort, you can continue on to the boil, just as you did when brewing from extract.

2 3
5 7

Part IV

The Rubber Meets the Road

Chapter 16

Homebrew Recipes

Omit and substitute! That's how recipes should be written.
Please don't ever get so hung up on published recipes
that you forget that you can omit and substitute.
– Jeff Smith, The Frugal Gourmet

THE FOLLOWING RECIPES SPAN A wide range of strength, from an Irish stout that, at 4.1 percent alcohol by volume (ABV), is on par with Bud Light (but far more flavorful) to an English barleywine whose more than 11 percent ABV will need several months' or years' aging to fully come into its own.

Each recipe includes a basic formulation built around extract and steeping grains. In all cases, the process is the same: Heat your steeping water to about 160–170°F (71–77°C), then kill the heat and add your mesh bag of crushed specialty grains. Wait half an hour, then remove the bag of grain, add the malt extract, turn the heat back on, and start the timer when boiling commences.

These recipes are written for full boils, which means starting with about 6.5 gallons (24.6 l) and ending up with 5.25 gallons (19.8 l) after 60 minutes of boiling. If you are boiling a smaller volume, such as in a stockpot on your kitchen stove, then divide the extract into early and late additions according to the fractional volume that you boil.

For example, if you begin with 3 gallons (11.3 l) and boil that down to 2.5 (9.5 l), then add only half of the malt extract before the boil and reserve the remainder for the final 10 minutes of the boil just for sanitation purposes. You don't have to get too precise with this:

You just want to avoid too concentrated a wort, which can affect hops utilization.

All recipes assume that you end up with 5.25 gallons (19.8 l) of wort at the end of the boil and that 0.25 gallons (946 ml) are lost to the fermentation process. Thus, 5 gallons (19 l) go into bottles or kegs when all is said and done. Feel free to adjust the amount of water you use if you find that you lose more or less liquid in the process.

The recipes also include all-grain formulations that assume 72 percent total brewhouse efficiency. No volume losses due to mash-lauter tun geometry, wort chiller, or other effects are included, since these vary so much from one system to the next. Take good notes on how much liquid you lose at each stage of the process and adjust your water volumes accordingly.

Some of the all-grain formulations include an optional multistep mash program (see Chapter 14). This is yours to take or leave as you see fit. The suggested single-temperature mash will always yield good results, but the optional mash regimens are provided for guidance should you want to experiment.

Unless otherwise indicated, the boil time for each recipe is 60 minutes. Exceptions to this are indicated in the individual recipes.

Two of these recipes—New Zealand IPA and Captain Cook's Strait Up DIPA—include first wort hops additions. First wort hopping (FWH) involves adding hops to the boil kettle while hot wort is run off from the lauter tun. Spending an hour or so steeping in hot runoff lends a hops character that some describe as especially smooth. If you're all-grain brewing, just plunk the first wort hops right into the boil kettle as you lauter and sparge, and leave them there for the duration of the boil.

Extract brewers can simulate the effect by adding hops to the hot steeping liquid after removing the steeping grains. If there are no steeping grains, just add the hops when the temperature of the water gets hot to the touch, around 150°F (66°C).

Good luck, and happy brewing!

O'Davey Irish Stout

Dry Irish Stout

OG: 1.045
FG: 1.013
IBUS: 48
ABV: 4.1%

EXTRACT & STEEPING GRAINS

6.5 lb (2.9 kg) Pale or Maris Otter liquid malt extract
1 lb (454 g) Weyermann Carafoam
1 lb (454 g) Simpsons Roasted Barley

HOPS SCHEDULE

2 oz (57 g) Willamette [6%] at 60 minutes

YEAST

Wyeast 1084 Irish Ale or
White Labs WLP004 Irish Ale Yeast

ALL-GRAIN RECIPE

6 lb (2.7 kg) Maris Otter
2 lb (907 g) Flaked Barley
1 lb (454 g) Simpsons Roasted Barley

Mash grains at 154°F (68°C) for 60 minutes.

Schaden-bräude Alt

Düsseldorf-style Altbier

OG: 1.047
FG: 1.013
IBUS: 49
ABV: 4.5%

EXTRACT & STEEPING GRAINS

6.5 lb (2.9 kg) Munich liquid malt extract
1 lb (454 g) Weyermann Caramunich I
2 oz (57 g) Weyermann Carafa Special II

HOPS SCHEDULE

0.6 oz (17 g) Magnum [12.5%] at 60 minutes
2 oz (57 g) Tettnang [4.5%] at 20 minutes

YEAST

Wyeast 1007 German Ale or White Labs WLP036 Düsseldorf Alt Yeast

ALL-GRAIN RECIPE

8 lb (3.6 kg) Weyermann Munich Type I
1 lb (454 g) Weyermann Caramunich I
2 oz (57 g) Weyermann Carafa Special II

Mash grains at 151°F (66°C) for 60 minutes, or if you're feeling adventurous, mash according to the following three-stage schedule:

Protein rest: 122°F (50°C) for 10 minutes
Saccharification: 150°F (66°C) for 45 minutes
Mash out: 170°F (77°C) for 10 minutes

BREWER'S NOTES

The suggested yeast strains are so-called hybrid strains that work best at a temperature somewhat between traditional ale and lager temperatures, usually around 60°F (16°C). If you can't find the suggested Alt strains, a Kölsch strain will work well, too. Try to keep fermentation cool, and you'll be rewarded with lager-like smoothness.

Weiße Katze Weißbier

Bavarian Hefeweizen

OG: 1.048
FG: 1.012
IBUS: 14
ABV: 4.6%

EXTRACT & STEEPING GRAINS

6.75 lb (3 kg) Wheat liquid malt extract
8 oz (227 g) Weyermann Carafoam

HOPS SCHEDULE

1 oz (28 g) Hallertauer Mittelfrüh [3.5%] at 60 minutes

YEAST

Wyeast 3068 Weihenstephan Weizen or White Labs WLP300 Hefeweizen Ale

ALL-GRAIN RECIPE

6.6 lb (2.9 kg) Wheat Malt
2.5 lb (1.1 kg) Weyermann Munich Type I
4 oz (113 g) Acidulated Malt

Mash grains at 152°F (67°C) for 60 minutes, or if you're feeling adventurous, mash according to the following four-stage schedule:

Protein rest: 122°F (50°C) for 10 minutes
Beta amylase: 145°F (63°C) for 30 minutes
Alpha amylase: 160°F (71°C) for 45 minutes
Mash out: 170°F (77°C) for 10 minutes

Citra Pale Nupti-Ale

An American Pale Ale served at the author's wedding to much acclaim

OG: 1.057
FG: 1.012
IBUS: 45
ABV: 5.9%

EXTRACT & STEEPING GRAINS
7.5 lb (3.4 kg) Pale liquid malt extract
12 oz (340 g) Caramel 60

HOPS SCHEDULE
1 oz (28 g) Chinook [13%] at 60 minutes
0.5 oz (14 g) Citra [12%] at 5 minutes
0.5 oz (14 g) Cascade [5.5%] at 5 minutes
0.5 oz (14 g) Citra [12%] at 0 minutes
0.5 oz (14 g) Cascade [5.5%] at 0 minutes
0.5 oz (14 g) Citra [12%] at dry hop 7 days
0.5 oz (14 g) Cascade [5.5%] at dry hop 7 days

YEAST
Wyeast 1056 American Ale,
White Labs WLP001 California Ale, or
Fermentis Safale US-05

ALL-GRAIN RECIPE
11 lb (4.9 kg) Pale Malt (2-Row)
12 oz (340 g) Caramel 60

Mash grains at 154°F (68°C) for 60 minutes.

Full Stop Stout

Dry Irish Stout

OG: 1.051
FG: 1.014
IBUS: 83
ABV: 4.8%

EXTRACT & STEEPING GRAINS
6.5 lb (2.9 kg) Maris Otter liquid malt extract
1 lb (454 g) Weyermann Carafoam
1.5 lb (680 g) Simpsons Roasted Barley
8 oz (227 g) Simpsons Black Malt

HOPS SCHEDULE
1 oz (28 g) Nugget [12.6%] at 60 minutes
1 oz (28 g) Galena [10.1%] at 30 minutes
1 oz (28 g) East Kent Goldings [4.7%] at 10 minutes

YEAST
Wyeast 1469 West Yorkshire Ale or
White Labs WLP007 Dry English Ale

ALL-GRAIN RECIPE
6.5 lb (2.9 kg) Maris Otter
2 lb (907 g) Flaked Barley
1.5 lb (680 g) Simpsons Roasted Barley
8 oz (227 g) Simpsons Black Malt

Mash grains at 152°F (67°C) for 60 minutes.

Schwarze Katze Dunkel

Dunkelweizen

OG: 1.052
FG: 1.014
IBUS: 16
ABV: 4.9%

EXTRACT & STEEPING GRAINS
4 lb (1.8 kg) Wheat liquid malt extract
3.5 lb (1.6 kg) Munich liquid malt extract
1 lb (454 g) Weyermann Caramunich II
2 oz (57 g) Weyermann Carafa Special II

HOPS SCHEDULE
1 oz (28 g) Hallertauer Mittelfrüh [4.3%] at 60 minutes

YEAST
Wyeast 3068 Weihenstephan Weizen or
White Labs WLP300 Hefeweizen Ale

ALL-GRAIN RECIPE
5 lb (2.3 kg) Weyermann dark wheat malt
4 lb (1.8 kg) Weyermann Munich Type I malt
1 lb (454 g) Weyermann Caramunich II
2 oz (57 g) Weyermann Carafa Special II

Mash grains at 152°F (67°C) for 60 minutes, or if you're feeling adventurous, mash according to the following four-stage schedule:

Protein rest: 122°F (50°C) for 10 minutes
Beta amylase: 145°F (63°C) for 30 minutes
Alpha amylase: 160°F (71°C) for 45 minutes
Mash out: 170°F (77°C) for 10 minutes

Throwback English IPA

English IPA

//

OG: 1.055
FG: 1.016
IBUS: 100
ABV: 5.1%

EXTRACT

8 lb (3.6 kg) Maris Otter liquid malt
  extract

HOPS SCHEDULE

3 oz (85 g) Willamette [6.00%] at
  60 minutes
2 oz (57 g) Fuggles [4.50%] at 30 minutes
2 oz (57 g) East Kent Goldings [4.70%]
  at 15 minutes
2 oz (57 g) East Kent Goldings [4.70%]
  at dry hop 7 days

YEAST

Mangrove Jack's Burton Union Yeast

ALL-GRAIN RECIPE

10.5 lb (4.76 kg) Maris Otter

Mash grains at 154°F (68°C) for 60
minutes.

Koriander und Salz, Gott erhalt's

Gose

//

OG: 1.052
FG: 1.013
IBUS: 14
ABV: 5.1%

EXTRACT & STEEPING GRAINS

7 lb 10 oz (3.46 kg) Wheat liquid malt extract
4 oz (113 g) Weyermann Carafoam

HOPS & SPICES SCHEDULE

0.5 oz (14 g) Perle [8%] at 45 minutes
1 oz (28 g) coriander seed at 10 minutes
0.5 oz (14 g) salt at 10 minutes

YEAST AND BACTERIA

Wyeast 5335 Lactobacillus
Wyeast 3068 Weihenstephan Weizen or
White Labs WLP300 Hefeweizen Ale

ALL-GRAIN RECIPE

6 lb (2.7 kg) Weyermann Wheat Malt
4 lb (1.8 kg) Weyermann Pilsner Malt

Mash grains at 146°F (63°C) for 90 minutes, or if you're feeling adventurous, mash
  according to the following three-stage schedule:

Protein rest: 122°F (50°C) for 10 minutes
Saccharification: 146°F (63°C) for 90 minutes
Mash out: 170°F (77°C) for 10 minutes

If you brew this as an all-grain beer, extend the boil from 60 to 90 minutes to drive
off dimethyl sulfide (DMS).

BREWER'S NOTES

To achieve the sour character for which Gose is so famous, first bring the wort
to a brief boil of 10 to 15 minutes without hops, then allow to cool to about 120°F
(49°C) in the kettle. Add the *Lactobacillus* directly in the kettle, and try to maintain
the temperature as near 120°F (49°C) as possible. Allow to sour for 24 hours. Then
bring to a boil and treat like a normal beer, adding the hops at the 45-minute
mark, and pitching the German wheat-beer strain after the cooled wort reaches
about 65°F (18°C).

Citrillo Wit

Witbier sans spices

///

OG: 1.053
FG: 1.013
IBUS: 21
ABV: 5.2%

EXTRACT & STEEPING GRAINS
7 lb 10 oz (3.46 kg) Wheat liquid malt extract
1 lb (454 g) Weyermann Carafoam

HOPS SCHEDULE
0.25 oz (7 g) Citra [12%] at 60 minutes
0.5 oz (14 g) Amarillo [8.5%] at 10 minutes
0.25 oz (7 g) Citra [12%] at 10 minutes
0.5 oz (14 g) Amarillo [8.5%] at 0 minutes
0.5 oz (14 g) Citra [12%] at 0 minutes

YEAST
Wyeast 3944 Belgian Witbier or
White Labs WLP400 Belgian Wit

ALL-GRAIN RECIPE
7 lb (3.2 kg) Pale Malt (2-Row)
3 lb (1.4 kg) Wheat Malt
8 oz (227 g) flaked oats

Mash grains at 150°F (66°C) for 60 minutes, or if you're feeling adventurous, mash according to the following three-stage schedule:

Protein rest: 122°F (50°C) for 10 minutes
Saccharification: 150°F (66°C) for 75 minutes
Mash out: 170°F (77°C) for 10 minutes

Mocktoberfest

Oktoberfest/Märzen-style ale

///

OG: 1.057
FG: 1.016
ABV: 5.4%
IBUS: 26

EXTRACT & STEEPING GRAINS
3 lb (1.4 kg) Munich liquid malt extract
5 lb (2.3 kg) Pilsner liquid malt extract
8 oz (227 g) Weyermann Carafoam

HOPS SCHEDULE
1 oz (28 g) Hallertauer Mittelfrüh [4%] at 60 minutes
1 oz (28 g) Hallertauer Mittelfrüh [4%] at 15 minutes

YEAST
Danstar Nottingham

ALL-GRAIN RECIPE
8 lb (3.6 kg) Weyermann Munich Type I
3 lb (1.4 kg) Weyermann Pilsner

Mash grains at 152°F (67°C) for 60 minutes, or if you're feeling adventurous, mash according to the following four-stage schedule:

Protein rest: 122°F (50°C) for 10 minutes
Beta amylase: 146°F (63°C) for 20 minutes
Alpha amylase: 158°F (70°C) for 30 minutes
Mash out: 170°F (77°C) for 10 minutes

Good Old Regular Pale Ale (GORP Ale)

American Pale Ale

///

OG: 1.053
FG: 1.012
IBUS: 39
ABV: 5.4%

EXTRACT & STEEPING GRAINS
7.75 lb (3.5 kg) Pale liquid malt extract
12 oz (340 g) Caramel 60

HOPS SCHEDULE
0.5 oz (14 g) Centennial [11.00 %] at 60 minutes
0.5 oz (14 g) Centennial [11.00 %] at 20 minutes
1 oz (28 g) Cascade [7.30 %] at 10 minutes
1 oz (28 g) Cascade [7.30 %] steep/whirlpool
1 oz (28 g) Cascade [7.30 %] at dry hop 7 days

YEAST
Wyeast 1056 American Ale,
White Labs WLP001 California Ale, or
Fermentis Safale US-05

ALL-GRAIN RECIPE
10 lb (4.5 kg) Pale Malt (2-Row)
12 oz (340 g) Caramel 60

Mash grains at 152°F (67°C) for 60 minutes.

O'Davey Irish Red

Irish Red Ale

OG: 1.056
FG: 1.013
IBUS: 28
ABV: 5.7%

EXTRACT & STEEPING GRAINS

8 lb (3.6 kg) Maris Otter liquid malt extract
6 oz (170 g) Crisp Light Crystal
4 oz (113 g) Simpsons Extra Dark Crystal
2 oz (57 g) Simpsons Dark Crystal
2 oz (57 g) Simpsons Roasted Barley

HOPS SCHEDULE

1 oz (28 g) Willamette [6%] at 60 minutes
1 oz (28 g) East Kent Goldings [4.7%] at 10 minutes

YEAST

Danstar Nottingham Yeast

ALL-GRAIN RECIPE

10 lb (4.5 kg) Maris Otter
6 oz (170 g) Crisp Light Crystal
4 oz (113 g) Simpsons Extra Dark Crystal
2 oz (57 g) Simpsons Dark Crystal
2 oz (57 g) Simpsons Roasted Barley

Mash grains at 152°F (67°C) for 60 minutes.

Festbier

Export-style Munich Helles

OG: 1.058
FG: 1.012
IBUS: 34
ABV: 6.1%

EXTRACT & STEEPING GRAINS

8.5 lb (3.85 kg) Pilsner liquid malt extract
4 oz (113 g) Weyermann Carafoam

HOPS SCHEDULE

1 oz (28 g) Perle [8%] at 60 minutes
1 oz (28 g) Hallertauer Mittelfrüh [4%] at 15 minutes

YEAST

Wyeast 2308 Munich Lager or
White Labs WLP835 German Lager X

ALL-GRAIN RECIPE

11 lb (4.9 kg) Weyermann Pilsner
4 oz (113 g) Acidulated Malt

Mash grains at 152°F (67°C) for 60 minutes, or if you're feeling adventurous, mash according to the following four-stage schedule:

Protein rest: 122°F (50°C) for 10 minutes
Beta amylase: 145°F (63°C) for 30 minutes
Alpha amylase: 160°F (71°C) for 45 minutes
Mash out: 170°F (77°C) for 10 minutes

If you brew this as an all-grain beer, extend the boil from 60 to 90 minutes to drive off dimethyl sulfide (DMS).

Paul Saison

Saison

OG: 1.057
FG: 1.005
IBUS: 34
ABV: 6.8%

EXTRACT & STEEPING GRAINS

6 lb (2.7 kg) Pilsner liquid malt extract
2.5 lb (1.1 kg) Wheat liquid malt extract

HOPS SCHEDULE

1 oz (28 g) Perle [8.6%] at 60 minutes
1 oz (28 g) Strisselspalt [2.5%] at 10 minutes
1 oz (28 g) Strisselspalt [2.5%] steep/whirlpool

YEAST

Wyeast 3711 French Saison or
Danstar Belle Saison

ALL-GRAIN RECIPE

8 lb (3.6 kg) Pilsner
2 lb (907 g) Weyermann Munich Type I
1 lb (454 g) Wheat Malt

Mash grains at 149°F (65°C) for 60 minutes.

If you brew this as an all-grain beer, extend the boil from 60 to 90 minutes to drive off dimethyl sulfide (DMS).

New Zealand IPA

American IPA featuring
New Zealand hops

////////////////////////////////////

OG: 1.063
FG: 1.014
IBUS: 86
ABV: 6.5%

EXTRACT & STEEPING GRAINS
9.5 lb (4.3 kg) Pale liquid malt extract
8 oz (227 g) Caramel 10
4 oz (113 g) Caramel 60

HOPS SCHEDULE
0.5 oz (14 g) Motueka [7%] at first wort
0.5 oz (14 g) Nelson Sauvin [12%] at
  first wort
0.5 oz (14 g) Rakau [10%] at first wort
0.5 oz (14 g) Motueka [7%] at 10 minutes
0.5 oz (14 g) Nelson Sauvin [12%] at
  10 minutes
0.5 oz (14 g) Rakau [10%] at 10 minutes
1 oz (28 g) Motueka [7%] at 5 minutes
1 oz (28 g) Rakau [10%] at 5 minutes
2 oz (57 g) Motueka [7%] at dry hop 7 days
2 oz (57 g) Rakau [10.5%] at dry hop 7 days

YEAST
Wyeast 1056 American Ale,
White Labs WLP001 California Ale, or
Fermentis Safale US-05

ALL-GRAIN RECIPE
12 lb (5.4 kg) Pale Malt (2-Row)
8 oz (227 g) Caramel 10
4 oz (113 g) Caramel 60

Mash grains at 152°F (67°C) for 60
minutes.

Do You Have a Flag?

English IPA

////////////////////////////////////

OG: 1.068
FG: 1.016
IBUS: 56
ABV: 6.9%

EXTRACT
10 lb (4.5 kg) Maris Otter liquid malt
extract

HOPS SCHEDULE
3 oz (85 g) Fuggles [5.1%] at 60 minutes
1 oz (28 g) East Kent Goldings [4.6%] at
  10 minutes
1 oz (28 g) East Kent Goldings [4.6%] at
  dry hop 7 days

YEAST
Mangrove Jack's Burton Union

ALL-GRAIN RECIPE
13 lb (5.9 kg) Maris Otter

Mash grains at 152°F (67°C) for 60
minutes.

Carpe Diem IPA

American IPA

////////////////////////////////////

OG: 1.069
FG: 1.015
IBUS: 70
ABV: 7.2%

EXTRACT & STEEPING GRAINS
10 lb 3 oz (4.6 kg) Pale liquid malt extract
1 lb (454 g) Caramel 40

HOPS SCHEDULE
1 oz (28 g) Magnum [12.5%] at 60 minutes
1 oz (28 g) Amarillo [9.2%] at 20 minutes
1.2 oz Simcoe [12.2%] at 5 minutes
1 oz (28 g) Amarillo [9.2%] at 0 minutes
1 oz (28 g) Amarillo [8.5%] at dry hop
  7 days
1 oz (28 g) Columbus [14%] at dry hop
  7 days
1 oz (28 g) Simcoe [13%] at dry hop 7 days

YEAST
Wyeast 1056 American Ale,
White Labs WLP001 California Ale, or
Fermentis Safale US-05

ALL-GRAIN RECIPE
13 lb (5.9 kg) Pale Malt (2-Row)
1 lb (454 g) Caramel 40

Mash grains at 152°F (67°C) for 60
minutes.

120/- Wee Heavy

Strong Scotch Ale

OG: 1.089
FG: 1.025
IBUS: 30
ABV: 8.5%

EXTRACT & STEEPING GRAINS

13 lb (5.9 kg) Maris Otter liquid malt extract
12 oz (340 g) Simpsons Medium Crystal
6 oz (170 g) Victory Malt
2 oz (57 g) Simpsons Extra Dark Crystal
2 oz (57 g) Crisp Roasted Barley

HOPS SCHEDULE

1.5 oz East Kent Goldings [6.3%] at
  60 minutes
0.5 oz East Kent Goldings [6.3%] at
  30 minutes

YEAST

Wyeast 1728 Scottish Ale Yeast or
White Labs WLP028 Edinburgh Ale

ALL-GRAIN RECIPE

16 lb (7.25 kg) Golden Promise
12 oz (340 g) Simpsons Medium Crystal
6 oz (170 g) Victory Malt
2 oz (57 g) Simpsons Extra Dark Crystal
2 oz (57 g) Crisp Roasted Barley

Mash grains at 154°F (68°C) for 75
minutes.

Vicar's Tipple

Belgian Tripel

OG: 1.082
FG: 1.012
IBUS: 25
ABV: 9.2%

EXTRACT

10 lb (4.5 kg) Pilsner liquid malt extract

HOPS & ADDITIONS SCHEDULE

1 oz (28 g) Styrian Goldings [5.4%] at
  60 minutes
0.5 oz (14 g) Hallertau Blanc [10%] at
  15 minutes
2.5 lb (1.1 kg) Simplicity Candi Syrup at
  10 minutes

YEAST

Wyeast 3787 Trappist High Gravity or
White Labs WLP530 Abbey Ale

ALL-GRAIN RECIPE

13 lb (5.9 kg) Pilsner Malt

Mash grains at 150°F (66°C) for
  75 minutes.

If you brew this as an all-grain beer,
extend the boil from 60 to 90 minutes
to drive off dimethyl sulfide (DMS).

Captain Cook's Strait Up DIPA

Imperial IPA

OG: 1.082
FG: 1.012
IBUS: 100
ABV: 9.3%

EXTRACT & STEEPING GRAINS

10 lb 11 oz (4.85 kg) Pale liquid malt extract
8 oz (227 g) Caramel 10
4 oz (113 g) Caramel 60
1 lb (454 g) corn sugar

HOPS SCHEDULE

1 oz (28 g) Motueka [7%] at first wort
1 oz (28 g) Rakau [10.5%] at first wort
0.5 oz (14 g) Nelson Sauvin [12%] at first
  wort
1 oz (28 g) Motueka [7%] at 10 minutes
1 oz (28 g) Rakau [10.5%] at 10 minutes
0.5 oz (14 g) Nelson Sauvin [12%] at
  10 minutes
1 oz (28 g) Motueka [7%] at 5 minutes
1 oz (28 g) Rakau [10.5%] at 5 minutes
1 oz (28 g) Motueka [7%] at 0 minutes
1 oz (28 g) Rakau [10.5%] at 0 minutes
2 oz (57 g) Motueka [7%] at dry hop 7 days
2 oz (57 g) Rakau [10.5%] at dry hop 7 days

YEAST

Wyeast 1056 American Ale,
White Labs WLP001 California Ale, or
Fermentis Safale US-05

ALL-GRAIN RECIPE

14 lb (6.35 kg) Pale Malt (2-Row)
8 oz (227 g) Caramel 10
4 oz (113 g) Caramel 60
1 lb (454 g) corn sugar

Mash grains at 150°F (66°C) for 60
minutes.

Mash Me if You Can

Wheatwine

//////////////////////////////

OG: 1.098
FG: 1.024
IBUS: 45
ABV: 9.8%

EXTRACT & STEEPING GRAINS
12 lb (5.4 kg) Wheat liquid malt extract
2 lb (907 g) corn sugar

HOPS SCHEDULE
1 oz (28 g) Nugget [12.6%] at 60 minutes
1 oz (28 g) Calypso [13%] at 10 minutes
1 oz (28 g) Calypso [13%] at 0 minutes

YEAST
Wyeast 1728 Scottish Ale or
  White Labs WLP028 Edinburgh Ale

ALL-GRAIN RECIPE
12 lb (5.4 kg) Wheat Malt
6 lb (2.7 kg) Pale Malt (2-Row)
12 oz (340 g) Caravienne Malt

Mash grains at 149°F (65°C) for 75 minutes.

The Invigilator

Doppelbock

//////////////////////////////

OG: 1.100
FG: 1.020
IBUS: 20
ABV: 10.6%

EXTRACT & STEEPING GRAINS
14 lb 5 oz (6.5 kg) Munich liquid malt extract
8 oz (227 g) Weyermann Caramunich II
4 oz (113 g) Weyermann Carafa Special II

HOPS SCHEDULE
1 oz (28 g) Perle [8%] at 60 minutes

YEAST
Wyeast 2487 Hella-Bock or White Labs
  WLP833 German Bock Lager

ALL-GRAIN RECIPE
12 lb (5.4 kg) Weyermann Munich Type I
6 lb (2.7 kg) Weyermann Munich Type II
8 oz (227 g) Weyermann Caramunich II
8 oz (227 g) Weyermann Melanoidin
4 oz (113 g) Weyermann Carafa Special II

Mash grains at 151°F (66°C) for 60 minutes.

Old Fussypants

English Barleywine

//////////////////////////////

OG: 1.109
FG: 1.025
IBUS: 63
ABV: 11.2%

EXTRACT & STEEPING GRAINS
13 lb (5.9 kg) Maris Otter liquid malt extract
2 lb (907 g) corn sugar
8 oz (227 g) Simpsons Caramalt
8 oz (227 g) Simpsons Medium Crystal

HOPS SCHEDULE
1.5 oz Magnum [12.5%] at 60 minutes
2 oz (57 g) East Kent Goldings [4%] at
  30 minutes
2 oz (57 g) East Kent Goldings [4%] at
  5 minutes

YEAST
Wyeast 1028 London Ale Yeast or
White Labs WLP013 London Ale

ALL-GRAIN RECIPE
20 lb (9.1 kg) Maris Otter
8 oz (227 g) Simpsons Caramalt
8 oz (227 g) Simpsons Medium Crystal

Mash grains at 152°F (67°C) for 60 minutes.

Epilogue

It alarms me to think of all that I have read and how little of it has stayed with me. – Hugh Laurie

IF EVER YOU NEED TO decide whether a person is truly brilliant or merely conceited and loud, here's my own personal litmus test: Bright individuals recognize that learning never ends, that it's impossible to know everything, and that all situations present a chance to discover something new.

What does this have to do with making beer? Everything and nothing, as it happens.

Most homebrewers you'll meet are kind, generous, passionate people who love what they do and want to share that enthusiasm with you. Spending time with a homebrewer can be as inviting as a warm hug. And if you drink enough home-brew, there's a real chance that hugs will commence before the evening is up, whether you want them or not.

But in any undertaking—whether it's brewing beer, designing a widget, or running for president—there are always those who claim to know everything, who insist that your way is wrong, and who refuse to consider other points of view. Unfortunately, it is a fundamental and inviolable truth of the universe that those who know the least tend to be the loudest.

Why do I bring this up? There's a great deal of incredible information out there for the eager homebrewer who wants to learn as much as he or she can, and I wholeheartedly encourage you to read as much as you can. But it's impossible to know all of it. Anyone who claims to have the right answer all the time should be viewed with a healthy degree of skepticism. Remember this piece of advice if ever you find yourself engaged in a heated debate on, say, the merits of the decoction mash.

Extend your skepticism to me, too. How many times have I stressed the importance of good sanitation in this book? Probably not as many as I should have. But if you discover, despite my advice, that you can brew great beer without paying attention to sanitation, then you should absolutely ignore me and—this is key—trust what you discover from firsthand experience. Your own experience as a homebrewer is, in the end, a far better guide for you than any book or celebrity, as long as you enjoy the results and have fun along the way.

Now, it's unlikely that you'll be able to get away with poor sanitation indefinitely because so many amateurs and professionals have brewed batches with flaws that can be directly attributed to less than stellar sanitation. There's a cause-and-effect relationship that, statistically speaking, will eventually find its way to you, too. If you're willing to accept the risk of some contaminated beer here and there, then that is your right to go against the grain. Conventional wisdom is a collection of suggestions, not sacred writ.

It's a bit of a silly example, but I hope it illustrates what I want you to take away from this book more than anything else: that homebrewing is a deeply personal experience and that your way of doing things can be just as valid as anyone else's. Maybe you'll buy a state-of-the-art, all-stainless brew rig, start winning competitions, and be well on your way to opening your own brewery soon. Or maybe you'll cobble together a basic homebrew kit and make just one batch every year at Thanksgiving with your uncle, a strong ale to open the next year and enjoy alongside the turkey. Both approaches are correct. Both are noble in their pursuits. And both deserve respect.

Why do I suddenly choose the epilogue to ruminate on the brewing of beer? Perhaps it is because homebrewing has given me far more than I would ever have expected. When I bought my first kit, my thinking was that maybe I would make some beer here and there. Maybe even just once. I didn't expect it to become so encompassing. And I certainly didn't expect to make it my career. But life is funny that way.

My sincerest hope is that this book ignites within you the curiosity and the courage to brew your own beer and to have fun doing so. I hope homebrewing gives you every bit as much cheer as it has given me. And I wish you many, many enjoyable glasses of homebrew to quench your thirst for making something hand-crafted and uniquely yours.

Cheers!

Brewing Glossary

acrospire – the barley shoot that develops during germination and malting.

adjunct – any non-enzymatic fermentable material that will feed the yeast. Common examples are rice, corn, refined sugar, raw wheat, flaked barley, and syrup.

ale – a beer brewed using a top-fermenting yeast at 60°–75°F (15°–24°C) for a relatively short time (2–3 weeks).

alpha acid – a class of chemical compounds found in hops cones' resin glands that is the source of hop bitterness.

amylase – an enzyme group that converts starch to sugar.

attenuation – the degree to which the fermentation process converts residual sugars to alcohol and CO_2.

autolysis – self-digestion and disintegration of yeast cells that can cause off-flavors if beer isn't racked from dead yeast after primary fermentation.

barley – cereal grain, member of the genus *Hordeum*. Malted barley is the primary ingredient in beer.

barrel – standard unit in commercial brewing. A U.S. barrel is 31.5 gallons; a British barrel is 43.2 U.S. gallons.

blow-off tube – a tube used during vigorous fermentation to allow the release of CO_2 and excess fermentation material.

Brettanomyces – colloquially referred to as *Brett,* a genus of yeast sometimes used in brewing. In a glucose-rich environment, it produces acetic acid.

chill haze – cloudy protein residue that precipitates when beer is chilled but re-dissloves as the beer warms up.

cold break – rapid precipitation of proteins that occurs when the wort is rapidly chilled before pitching the yeast.

conditioning – a term for secondary fermentation, in which the beer matures.

cone – the part of the hops plant used in brewing.

corn sugar – dextrose. Sometimes added as an adjunct in beer to raise alcohol percentage and lighten the color of the beer.

diacetyl – a powerful flavor chemical with the aroma of butter or butterscotch.

dimethyl sulfide (DMS) – a powerful flavor chemical found in beer, with the aroma of cooked corn or cabbage.

dry-hopping – adding hops directly to the fermentor at the end of fermentation to increase hop aroma without adding bitterness.

endosperm – the starchy middle of a barley grain that is the source of fermentable material for brewing.

enzymes – proteins that act as catalysts for most reactions crucial to brewing, including starch conversion and yeast metabolism.

esters – aromatic compounds formed from yeast's complete oxidation of various alcohols and responsible for most fruity aromas in beer.

ethanol – the type of alcohol found in beer, formed by yeast from malt sugars.

extract – concentrated wort in dry or syrup form.

fermentation – yeast's biochemical process involving the metabolism of sugars and the release of CO_2 and alcohol.

final gravity (FG) – measure of beer strength after fermentation is complete, expressed as specific gravity.

finings – clarifying agents added to wort or beer to help pull suspended yeast, malt proteins, and polyphenols out of the beer.

first runnings – the first few quarts of wort that are drained off at the beginning of runoff until the draining wort is fairly clear.

flocculation – the clumping together and settling of the yeast out of solution.

FWH – "first wort hopping" is a process that involves adding finishing hops to the boil kettle as the wort is drained from the lauter or mash tun.

grist – ground grain ready for brewing.

hops – a climbing vine of the Cannabacinae family, whose cones are used to give beer its bitterness and characteristic aroma.

hot break – (also known as hot trub) the rapid coagulation of proteins and tannins that forms a brown scum on top of the wort as the boil begins.

husk – the outer covering of barley or other grains.

hydrometer – a glass instrument used in brewing to measure the specific gravity of beer and wort to calculate alcohol percentage and fermentation status.

IBU (international bittering unit) – the accepted method of expressing hop bitterness in beer.

infusion – a mashing technique where heating is accomplished with addition of boiling water.

Irish moss (also called carrageen) – a marine algae used to promote the formation of break material and precipitation during the boil.

iso-alpha acid – predominant source of bitterness in beer. Derived from the hops during the boil.

kettle – boiling vessel, also known as a copper.

Kräeusen – the thick foamy head on fermenting beer.

lactic acid – a tart, sour acid that is a by-product of *Lactobacillus.*

Lactobacillus – large genus of bacteria. Some species are used in the production of yogurt, sauerkraut, pickles, and sour beers.

lactose – an unfermentable sugar that comes from milk. Traditionally used in milk stout.

lag time – adaptation phase after the yeast is pitched during which the yeast begins a period of rapid aerobic growth.

lager – a beer brewed with a bottom-fermenting yeast between 45°–55°F (7°–13°C) and given 4–6 weeks to ferment.

lautering – a process in which the mash is separated into the liquid wort and the residual grain.

lauter tun – traditional vessel used to separate the wort from the residual grains.

lightstruck – a skunky off-flavor in beer that develops from exposure to short-wavelength light.

malt – barley or other grain that has been allowed to sprout, then dried or roasted.

mash – the hot-water steeping process in which starch is converted into sugars.

mash tun – vessel with a false bottom in which mashing is carried out.

melanoidins – the strong flavor compounds produced by Maillard browning.

milling – grinding or crushing grain.

modification – the degree to which the protein-starch matrix breaks down during malting.

mouthfeel – sensory qualities of a beer other than flavor, such as body and carbonation.

original gravity (OG) – measure of wort strength before yeast is added, expressed as specific gravity.

oxidation – chemical reaction that occurs between oxygen and various components in beer.

parti-gyle – to get multiple beers out of the same mash. The brewer boils successive runnings separately and, ideally, blends them to different strengths.

Pediococcus – bacteria similar to *Lactobacillus* that produces lactic acid. *Pedio* is less sensitive to hops and can work at lower pH levels than *Lacto*,

so most of the lactic-acid character in sour ales comes from *Pedio*.

pH (potential of hydrogen) – the scale used to express the level of acidity and alkalinity in a solution in a water-based solution. Neutral pH in water has a value of 7; most acidic is a value of 0; most alkaline is a value of 14.

phenol – chemical family responsible for spicy, smoky, clove-like, and other aromas in beer.

pitch – adding yeast to the fermentor.

polishing – final filtration before bottling

ppm – parts per million. Most commonly used to express dissolved mineral concentrations in water.

primary fermentation – initial rapid stage of yeast activity when maltose and other simple sugars are metabolized.

priming – adding a small amount of sugar to beer before bottling to restart fermentation and give the beer carbonization.

protein – complex organic molecules involved in enzyme activity, yeast nutrition, head retention, and colloidal stability.

protein rest – during mashing, a rest that allows remnant large proteins to be broken down into smaller proteins and amino acids and any remaining starches to be released from the endosperm.

racking – carefully siphoning the beer away from the trub to another fermentor or to bottles.

Reinheitsgebot – Bavarian beer-purity law, enacted in 1516 decreeing that beer can have only three components: water, barley, and hops. Yeast was added later.

runnings – wort that is drained from the mash during sparging.

saccharification – conversion of starch to sugars in the mash through enzymatic action.

Saccharomyces – scientific genus

name of brewer's yeast.

sanitize – to reduce microbial contaminants to insignificant levels.

secondary fermentation – after the primary fermentation, beer is racked to a sterile container for a slower phase of yeast activity during which complex sugars are metabolized.

sparge – rinsing mashed grains with hot water to recover all available wort sugars.

specific gravity – the ratio of the density of a solution to standard solution, such as water, at a defined temperature.

starch – complex carbohydrates that are converted into sugars during mashing.

steep – soaking barley or wheat in water to begin malting.

step mash – mashing technique that uses controlled temperature steps.

sterilize – to eliminate all forms of life by either chemical or physical means.

strike – adding hot water to the crushed malt to raise the temperature and begin mashing.

tannins – polyphenols, complex organic materials with an astringent flavor, extracted from barley husks and hops.

trub – the hot and cold break material, hop bits, and dead yeast sediment at the bottom of the fermentor.

whirlpool – a device that separates the hops and trub from the wort after boiling.

wine thief – an instrument used for taking a sample of wine or beer from a fermentor.

wort – the sugar-laden liquid from the mash.

wort chiller – a heat exchanger that rapidly cools wort from near boiling to pitching temperatures.

yeast – a large class of microscopic fungi, several species of which are used in brewing.

Index

Index